Test Your Professional English

Marketing

Simon Sweeney

Series Editor: Nick Brieger

PENGUIN ENGLISH

To Mum and Dad with love

Pearson Education Limited
Edinburgh Gate
Harlow
Essex CM20 2JE, England
and Associated Companies throughout the world.

ISBN 0 582 45150 7

First published 1996 under the title *Test Your Business English: Marketing*
Text copyright © Simon Sweeney, 1996, 2000, 2002

Designed and typeset by Pantek Arts Ltd, Maidstone, Kent
Test Your format devised by Peter Watcyn-Jones
Illustrations by Roger Fereday and Anthony Seldon
Printed in Italy by Rotolito Lombarda

Acknowledgements
The following people helped me prepare the first edition of this book, and I extend warmest thanks to each of them: Steve Flinders, Steve Hick, John Hinman, Barry Jones, Clare Munden and John Murphy. I would also like to thank colleagues and friends in the School of Management, Community and Communication at York St John College, especially Andy Hutchings. Thanks too to Nick Brieger, the series editor. I am particulary grateful to Helen Parker and colleagues at Penguin English. Helen made many useful suggestions, leading to considerable improvements on my early draft. Christine Lindop did an excellent job in preparing the final manuscript. Thanks to all the above, with the usual plea that they should in no way be held responsible for any remaining weaknesses. Over those, I claim sole ownership.

Published by Pearson Education Limited in association with Penguin Books Ltd, both companies being subsidiaries of Pearson plc.

For a complete list of the titles available from Penguin English please visit our website at www.penguinenglish.com, or write to your local Pearson Education office or to: Marketing Department, Penguin Longman Publishing, 80 Strand, London WC2R 0RL.

Contents

Section 7: Consumers and market segmentation

Section 8: Planning and international marketing

To the student

Do you use English in your work or in your studies? Maybe you are already working in business, perhaps directly in marketing. Or perhaps you are studying a course in business studies, management or marketing. If you need to improve your knowledge of marketing and marketing terms, this book will help you. You can check your knowledge of basic marketing concepts, key words and essential expressions so that you can communicate more effectively and confidently in your work and for your studies.

There are eight sections in the book. The first section is an introduction to general marketing terms and concepts. The remaining seven sections each cover a different area of marketing, including core areas such as product, price and promotion, as well as research, planning and international marketing. You can either work through the book from beginning to end or select chapters according to Your interests and needs.

Many tests also have useful tips (advice) on language learning or further professional information. The tips offer important extra help.

Many different kinds of tests are used, including sentence transformation, gap-filling, word families, multiple choice, crosswords and short reading texts. There is a key at the back of the book so that you can check your answers; and a word list to help you revise key vocabulary.

Your vocabulary is an essential resource for effective communication. The more words you know, the more meanings you can express. This book will help you develop your specialist vocabulary still further. Using the tests you can check what you know and also learn new concepts and new words, all related to the field of marketing, in a clearly structured framework.

Simon Sweeney

The full series consists of:

Test Your Professional English: Accounting	Alison Pohl
Test Your Professional English: Business General	Steve Flinders
Test Your Professional English: Business Intermediate	Steve Flinders
Test Your Professional English: Finance	Simon Sweeney
Test Your Professional English: Hotel and Catering	Alison Pohl
Test Your Professional English: Law	Nick Brieger
Test Your Professional English: Management	Simon Sweeney
Test Your Professional English: Marketing	Simon Sweeney
Test Your Professional English: Medical	Alison Pohl
Test Your Professional English: Secretarial	Alison Pohl

1 Definitions

Fill each gap in the sentences below with the correct word from the box.

> customers   developing   distribute   needs   place   price   producing
> ~~product~~   product   profit   promote   service   time   want

Marketing is concerned with getting the right (1) ____*product*____ to the right (2) _____ at the right (3) _____ .

Marketing is about meeting consumer (4) _____ at a (5) _____ .

Marketing makes it easier for (6) _____ to do business with you[1].

Marketing aims to find out what people (7) _____ ; then (8) _____ and (9) _____ a (10) _____ or (11) _____ that will satisfy those wants; and then determining the best way to (12) _____ (13) _____ and (14) _____ the product or service[2].

 Here is another definition. 'Marketing is the management process responsible for identifying, anticipating and satisfying customer requirements profitably'[3].
Which of these definitions is/are most closely related to your view of marketing?

[1] Booth D., *Principles of Strategic Marketing*, Tudor Publishing, 1990
[2] Stanton W.J., *Fundamentals of Marketing*, McGraw Hill, 1981
[3] Chartered Institute of Marketing, quoted in Hannagan T., *Management: Concepts and Practices*, Financial Times / Pitman Publishing, 1998

2 Key words 1

A Find eleven common words connected with marketing in the word square. Four of them are vertical, six are horizontal, and one is diagonal.

R	Q	A	I	J	K	L	M	P	L	A	N
C	U	S	T	O	M	E	R	S	P	O	Q
A	A	S	M	A	R	K	E	T	I	N	G
H	L	D	L	F	G	H	J	T	S	T	O
O	I	E	E	F	W	R	U	U	C	V	O
J	T	M	A	G	Y	B	B	C	E	A	D
L	Y	A	T	H	I	R	U	B	D	U	S
N	Q	N	P	R	O	D	U	C	T	Q	P
O	S	D	T	T	R	V	G	H	J	W	R
O	M	S	E	R	V	I	C	E	S	X	E
D	I	K	I	R	E	S	E	A	R	C	H
D	X	X	A	P	Q	U	A	N	A	F	H

B Use words from the square to complete the text below.

Marketers and all levels of management realise the vital importance of 1) _____ . This has become the watchword of good business. 2) _____ and experience has shown that 3) _____ will pay more for 4) _____ and 5) _____ of high quality, and also that they expect every aspect of the 6) _____ , including 7) _____ , to meet the highest standards. The job of marketers is to design a 8) _____ 9) _____ with a 10) _____ of all the necessary components to satisfy consumer 11) _____ .

C Find words in your completed text in B that mean the same as the following:

1 users of products and services

2 people who buy products and services

3 business professionals who work in the field of marketing

4 studies

5 the extent to which consumers want something

6 the movement of goods and services from the producer to the consumer

7 the combination of factors that makes up a marketing plan

Many marketing words are part of everyday language. Which of the words above are now in common use? What other marketing words do you know that are like this?

3 Word building

A Fill in the missing words in the table.

	Verb	Agent	General noun
1	*market*	marketer	
2	distribute		
3			competition
4			advertising advertisement
5		supplier	
6		sponsor	
7	consume		
8	produce		
9		analyst	
10		researcher	
11	import		

B   Complete the sentences below with words from the word table.

1   Marketers m_____ p_____ to customers.

2   Advertisers a_____ to c_____ .

3   Market analysts a_____ the performance of s_____ and the behaviour of c_____ .

4   The opposite of export is _____ .

5   The opposite of demand is _____ .

6   C_____ is good for consumers.

7   S_____ is a form of a_____ .

- A word table is a useful tool for increasing your vocabulary. Make a table of your own with new vocabulary; look for related forms, i.e. nouns, verbs, adjectives and adverbs.
- The nouns *imports* and *exports* are usually used in the plural. **Invisible exports** means financial services, banking, insurance and tourism, where these bring in money from foreign countries.

---

[1] The term **marketeer** is used in marketing magazines and by people in the business, but in general use **marketer** is more common. The most popular term, however, is *marketing person/people*.

[2] con-man – someone who tricks people into spending money

4 Marketing, marketing people and markets

| A | For each definition choose the correct word or phrase. |

1 Providing money to cultural or sporting activities in exchange for advertising rights.
a) promotion   b) grant aid   ⓒ sponsorship

2 A business which specializes in giving advice and support to companies about marketing and markets.
a) marketing consultancy   b) counselling service
c) company analysts

3 An economy which allows open and reasonably free exchange between private companies.
a) command economy   b) conservative economy
c) free market economy

4 A market in which there are too many suppliers producing similar products.
a) saturated market   b) buyers' market   c) heavy market

5 A market in which there are few suppliers producing goods that a lot of people want to buy.
a) weak market   b) sellers' market   c) light market

6 A company which sells more of a particular type of product than its competitors.
a) trend setter   b) multinational   c) market leader

7 A person who uses their specialist knowledge of a specific market to try to explain what has happened and predict what will happen.
a) market analyst   b) forecaster   c) market broker

8 A specific promotional activity over a limited period of time.
a) campaign   b) season   c) trend

9 The activity of moving goods from the producer to the consumer.
a) selling   b) distribution   c) orientation

10 The activity of selling goods to other countries.
a) multinational   b) exporting   c) exchange distribution

11 The proportion of the total market which one company controls.
a) dominion   b) market place   c) market share

12 What a company or organization says it intends to do for its customers/clients and the community.
a) corporate mission   b) strategic plan   c) corporate image

B Match each picture below to one of the terms above.

1

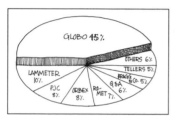

2

3

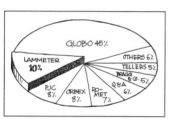

4

5

• Practise using the words you learn so they become active vocabulary. For example, choose six words from this test that you did not know before and write a sentence using each one.

• Diamonds are a classic example of a **sellers' market**. There is a lot of demand for the product but there are very few **suppliers**. That's why diamonds are rare and extremely expensive!

5 The four Ps and three more Ps

Fill in the missing words in this description of the marketing mix.

The traditional marketing mix was described in terms of four Ps:

1   P r o d u c t, the goods or services

2   P _ _ _ _ , the cost of the product

3   P _ _ _ _ , often called distribution

4   P _ _ _ _ _ _ _ _ , which aims to make people aware of the product.

In recent years other considerations have been added, giving a mix of normally seven Ps. The additional three, sometimes referred to as service Ps are:

5   P _ _ _ _ _ , or everyone involved from producer to consumer

6   P _ _ _ _ _ _ _ e _ _ _ _ _ _ _ _ , or anything that shows the existence of the company, e.g. its buildings, vehicles, website, stationery, staff uniforms, badges.

7   P _ _ _ _ _ _ , which is the interaction between *everyone* involved.

The last P is an increasingly important part of training nowadays. Companies and organizations must be sure that their product or service reaches the customer in the most efficient and effective way.

6 Planning

Look at the flyer below advertising marketing strategy seminars. Fill each gap with the correct word from the box.

> mix   opportunities   people   physical evidence   place
> ~~plan~~   price   process   product   promotion
> strengths   threats   weaknesses

SANDERMAN & KELLS ASSOCIATES
– Business Strategists –
Marketing is Our Business

MARKETING SEMINARS – Corachie Park Hotel, Taynuilt, Oban, Strathclyde

Seminars throughout March, July and November 2001.

Success depends on good marketing. Your business needs a clear strategy to develop understanding of:
1. your present position and the market environment
2. the best marketing strategy to reach your customers and build profits for your business

Any business must have a marketing (1) _____*plan*_____. This should be based on a clear SWOT analysis, i.e. understanding of the present market position in terms of:
- (2) _____
- (3) _____
- (4) _____
- (5) _____

The seminar will examine ways to develop a seven-point marketing (6) _____ consisting of:

- (7) _____
- (8) _____
- (9) _____
- (10) _____
- (11) _____
- (12) _____
- (13) _____ _____

Send for details and an application form now to Andrew G. Boscher, Chief Executive Marketing, Sanderman & Kells Associates, PO Box 2001, Edinburgh EB12 7TR
or by email to andyboscher@sandkells.co.uk

---

7 The marketing mix

Peter Bowen of Citimetal Inc. is talking to Anna James, a marketing consultant. Complete Anna's part of the conversation. Choose from the following:

a And then the fourth area is physical evidence.

b It covers both goods and services offered by the company.

c Exactly – and the desire to buy the product. And, finally, people, which means colleagues, employees, agents and customers. The idea is to keep everyone happy, make personal contact.

d Yes. This means any visual presence or signs suggesting the company.

e The second area is place – also called distribution – meaning the movement of goods from the producer to the consumer.

f Well, we identified six areas where improvement is necessary.

g After place, process. Process is the interaction between people and systems at all stages, from market research, design, production, delivery and after-sales.

h The first is product.

i Promotion.

Peter: So, what have you got to report?

Anna: _____

_____

Peter: Really? What are they?

Anna: _____

_____

Peter: And what exactly does that term cover?

Anna: _____

_____

Peter: I see. What else?

Anna: _____

_____

Peter: And after place, what's next?

Anna: _____

_____

Peter: Yes, I understand – co-ordination of systems.

Anna: _____

_____

Peter: Physical evidence?

Anna: _____

_____

Peter: Everything visual. Right, I follow you. And what's the next area?

Anna: _____

_____

Peter: So, that's creating consumer awareness and establishing the brand identity?

Anna: _____

_____

- Notice which Ps are not included in the conversation above (Price and Process).
- A good way to learn vocabulary is to use real-life examples. Think of a famous company and give examples of its Ps in a marketing mix.

8 A new market

M & T Cables wants to enter a new market. Read the following email to a possible export partner. Fill each gap in the sentences below with the correct word from the box.

analysis	demand	free	~~goods~~	mix	plan	research	trends

Date 22 Nov 2000 15:48:45 +0900
From: M & T Cables GmbH <MTCables@worldcom.de>
To: 'Peter Jarrow' PDJARROW@gold.ocn.fi
Subject: Export proposal

Dear Peter,

Thanks for your letter about marketing our products in the South Pacific region. We certainly do want to sell our (1) __*goods*__ in every (2) _____ market in the world, but we need to do some market (3) _____ in your region.

I have four questions to start with:

1. What is the supply and (4) _____ like at present for our kind of products?
2. What kind of (5) _____ do you think we should develop in our marketing (6) _____ ?
3. What are the market (7) _____ in this sector?
4. Can you recommend someone to carry out a detailed market (8) _____ for us?

Please email by return if possible. Thank you!

Sandra Sah

Lindacher Str. 48. D-40474 Düsseldorf. Germany
MTCables@worldcom.de
Tel: 0049 211 646453 or 646458. Fax: 0049 211 646460

---

9 Product marketing

Choose the best definition for each of the words or phrases.

1 augmented product
   a) a product now selling at a higher price
   b) a product that is no longer made
   c) a core product plus additional benefits such as brand name, quality styling and design features, extended warranty, after-sales service, etc.

2 generic
   a) not known by a special brand name
   b) for general use
   c) popular with all types of consumers

3 cannibalism
   a) when a product eats into the competitors' market share
   b) when a product reduces sales of other products made by the same manufacturer
   c) when an employee leaves his/her company to join a competitor

4 sell-by date
   a) the limit placed on sales representatives to meet targets
   b) the date by which a food or drug must be sold
   c) the date on which a product is sold

5 launch
   a) when a product is taken off the market
   b) when a product is tested before being sold
   c) when a product is first released onto the market

6 product life cycle
   a) the normal pattern of sales for a product
   b) the process of development of a new product
   c) the different stages of improvement in an old product

7 part
   a) a product
   b) a component
   c) a phase in the development of a product

10 Branding

A Rearrange the letters to make words and phrases that are connected with branding.

1 nbard yitnedit _brand identity_

2 ardnb eman _____

3 dabrn igema _____

4 won-drabn _____

5 radbn nataviluo _____

6 burnadden _____

7 antilbinge stases _____

8 andrb yallyot _____

9 rempuim bdarn _____

B Complete each sentence with the correct word or phrase from A.

1 Coca Cola, Sony, Mercedes Benz: each of these is a famous

_____ .

2 Deciding a financial value for a brand name is called

_____ .

3 Consumers usually expect to pay less for products that are

_____ .

4 Products like Chanel or Christian Dior have a
_____ which is more glamorous than that of many
less well-known competitors.

5 In the 1990s most supermarkets began to sell
_____ products.

6 A brand name is valuable not only for the main products that are
represented by the name, but also for the range of
_____ that accompany that name.

7 A key concern for marketers is to establish _____ among their customers so that they do not buy similar products made by other companies.

8 Consumers are often prepared to pay a high price for a _____ which they believe represents high quality.

9 A new product must create a _____ so that it is easily recognized and associated with specific qualities.

 The greatest single change in marketing in recent years has been the growth in importance of **brands** and **branding**. **Brand strength** is often a more important factor in company valuations than **physical assets**. These days it is often brands and brand names that attract **take-overs**, rather than physical assets or access to particular markets.

11 Key words 2

Next to each word or phrase write the number of the correct picture (1–10) and the letter of the correct description (a–j).

augmented product   _7e_   generic product   _____

clone   _____   perishables   _____

consumer durable   _____   manufacturing   _____

core product   _____   sell-by date   _____

fast moving   service   _____
consumer goods   _____

a   Natural products, usually food, that will go bad after a certain length of time.

b   Products sold in very large quantities, such as groceries. They are bought often and move through stores quickly.

c   A new product, especially in the high technology sector, which is almost the same as a successful one made by a more famous manufacturer.

d   Long-lasting products produced and sold in large quantities.

e   A basic product with additional features and services added to the total package.

f   A basic product which is bought because of a particular need, e.g. a drink for thirst.

g   Products which are not known by a brand name, e.g. pharmaceutical products like paracetamol for headaches.

h   Specialist expertise or advice to help companies or individuals, e.g. in legal matters, marketing.

i   A time suggested for reasons of safety by which perishable goods should be used.

j   The actual making of products or components for products.

The term **clone**, meaning an exact copy, has become part of popular speech. The science of cloning, using genetic material to develop new organisms, has caused controversy in recent years. In Britain scientists produced a cloned sheep called Dolly. She is probably the most famous sheep in history!

12 Selling

Jan Groot, Marketing Manager for TPC Inc., is making a presentation to the company's sales staff. Match each picture with the correct part of the speech and write its number in the box.

Our R & D department designed the Triple X Pathway over a five-year period ...

5

... and the product was finally launched this year.

The core product is, of course, a personal computer ...

... but the augmented package includes ten types of software, a DVD drive, speakers, a printer, a scanner, manuals, free Internet access, free on-site warranty and the prestige of the Triple X brand name.

5

Of course, all components used in the manufacture of the Triple X Pathway have been well tested.

☐

6

We offer a full after-sales service ...

☐

7

... and extended five-year warranty with absolute confidence.

☐

8

Furthermore, we expect the product to experience rapid early sales for at least three years ...

☐

9

... before being joined by me-too products from our competitors.

☐

13 Product management

A A useful tool in product management is the idea of Product Life Cycle. The diagram shows a typical product life cycle. Label the parts 1–6 with words from the box.

| decline | development | growth | launch | maturity | saturation |

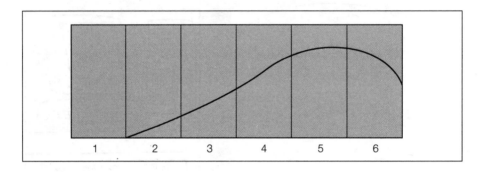

B Complete the sentences with terms from the box.

appeal	consumers	decision-making	development	extend
markets	penetration	portfolio	positioning	~~potential~~
	quality	research	return	

1 Managers have to understand the ___*potential*___ of their products.

2 Most companies produce many different products and services. Together this is called the product _____ .

3 Companies market products at particular groups of consumers, so the product is matched to the consumer. This is called product _____ .

4 Product management is about getting the maximum _____ from each product.

5 A key objective is to get the maximum market ＿＿＿＿＿＿ ,
which means reaching the most ＿＿＿＿＿＿ .

6 Another important objective is to ＿＿＿＿＿＿ the life of the
product. The typical life cycle diagram then shows a wave effect.

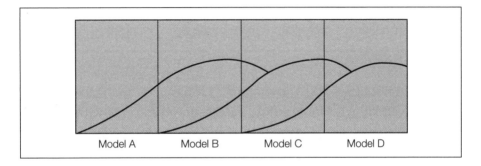

Model A   Model B   Model C   Model D

7 This is possible if the product ＿＿＿＿＿＿ is good. This
means changing or improving the product, to add to its
＿＿＿＿＿＿ and ＿＿＿＿＿＿ .

8 Managers also try to find new ＿＿＿＿＿＿ for their products.

9 In all cases, product management needs good ＿＿＿＿＿＿ to
help ＿＿＿＿＿＿ .

- A classic **life cycle** from development to decline is demonstrated by
  fashion items (such as toys that are spin-off products from the movie
  industry) or by technology products that were once **state-of-the-art** but
  are later replaced by technological innovation (such as early fax machines).
  Products at the end of their life cycle are described as **obsolescent**.

- One of Europe's most successful cars ever is the Volkswagen Golf. Since it
  was first launched it has experienced many **face-lifts** (improvements that
  mostly affect appearance). After each face-lift the car looked different.
  Nowadays the car is still an outstanding product and it looks radically different
  from the original Golf. This is a good example of an **extended life cycle**.

14 After-sales assistance

The following text came with the user manual for a new telephone. Fill each gap with the correct word or phrase from the box.

after-sales	customer	helpline	labour	~~launched~~	network
on-site	parts	premium	state-of-the-art	support	warranty

Since the TeleTalk was (1) __*launched*__ , it has been an outstanding success. Well known for reliability, it does, however, come with a full two-year (2) _____ and (3) _____ (4) _____.

Utilizing the very latest technology, this (5) _____ product is supported by our extensive (6) _____ (7) _____ . Call our (8) _____ (9) _____ for free advice on how to solve any problems you may have. For a small (10) _____ we can also offer a full (11) _____ technical (12) _____ service for all your communications equipment.

'...all our operators are busy. Please hold and we'll try to connect you...'

 Most products, when new, come with a **leaflet** in the box. This is often printed in several languages. Find an example and look at the English version. Use the leaflet to make vocabulary learning notes.

15 Products, services and service

Change each word in bold type to a related word which fills the gap in the sentence correctly.

1 We sell a very large range of goods, including fast moving ____*consumer*____ goods such as canned foods, cleaning materials and cassettes.   **consume**

2 Of course, we also sell _____ goods like milk, cheese and meat, which need to be sold within a short time.   **perish**

3 It is not only food _____ which have a very short shelf life. Fashion items quickly become out of date.   **produce**

4 For larger consumer _____ , like music systems and TVs, we provide an after-sales service.   **duration**

5 An important aspect of marketing goods like computers is possible _____ value, such as free software, Internet access and technical support.   **add**

6 The business of a _____ is to sell products.   **retail**

7 A _____ industry is one that offers specialist expertise or advice. Lawyers, marketers, translators and financial consultants all do this.   **serve**

8 If you are not completely satisfied with any product _____ in this store, you may return it and receive a complete refund or exchange it for a different item.   **purchaser**

9 A _____ gives one person or company the right to make a particular product for a period of time. The inventor may sell or lease it to a manufacturer.   **patented**

10 A product which was expensive to develop, manufacture and launch, and which does not have the sales that the manufacturer expected can be described as a _____ .   **flopped**

16 Success and failure

Fill each gap in the sentences with the correct word from the box.

away	back	by	into	~~off~~	on	on	to

1 Perishable goods go ____*off*____ in a short time.

2 If dairy products are not sold _____ the sell-by date, they cannot be offered for sale.

3 Unsold perishable goods usually have to be thrown _____ .

4 If a safety fault is discovered in a product, the manufacturer may ask customers to bring _____ all examples of the product.

5 Thousand of new products are put _____ the market every day, but only a few are successful.

6 Success or failure depends _____ many factors, but the most important is the quality of the marketing.

7 Customers with a strong sense of brand loyalty are rarely prepared to switch _____ a competitor.

8 Powerful advertising may help a new product to eat _____ the market share of rival brands.

If a **safety fault** is found in products after they have been sold, the manufacturers usually issue a **product recall**. They put notices in the shops where the product is sold, and/or announcements in newspapers, asking customers to bring back the product for a repair, replacement or refund. Product recalls can involve a lot of work and cost a lot of money!

17 Key words 3

A Find eight common words connected with price in the word square. Four of the words are horizontal, and four are vertical (two up and two down).

A	P	R	I	C	E	L	T
D	I	S	C	O	U	N	T
E	C	R	G	S	N	O	I
M	P	O	R	T	E	V	F
A	W	R	M	S	V	I	O
N	I	P	F	E	E	O	R
D	R	L	M	H	R	G	P
A	M	A	R	G	I	N	E

B Use one word from the word square to complete each sentence.

1 When a business pays all its costs and taxes, any money left is _____profit_____ .

2 Another word for income is _____ .

3 The difference between costs and selling price is the

_____ .

4 Many consumers normally look for the lowest _____ .

5 Selling something at a reduced price is called giving a

_____ .

6 The price you pay for a professional service, for example from an architect, doctor or lawyer, is a _____ .

7 Businesses can't sell products if there is no _____ .

8 Another word for expenses is _____ .

Write PRICE in the middle of a large piece of paper. Then add the other key words from this exercise. As you study this section, write all the new words you learn on the paper to create a web of price-related terms. You can use this learning tip for other themes as well.

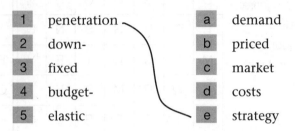

18 Fixing a price

A   Match each word on the left with a word on the right to create a two-word phrase connected with pricing.

1	penetration	a	demand
2	down-	b	priced
3	fixed	c	market
4	budget-	d	costs
5	elastic	e	strategy

B   Now make five two-word expressions which are opposite in meaning to those in A.

1	inelastic	a	demand
2	variable	b	priced
3	premium-	c	market
4	skimming	d	costs
5	up-	e	strategy

C   Find the correct term from A or B to complete each sentence below.

1   Where sales are not affected much by price rises, this is _____ .

2   Selling widely in a market for low profit per item is a _____

3   High quality, high-priced products are _____

4   A company accounts term meaning the cost of things like electricity, rent, and other charges that do not increase with increases in production is _____ .

5   Low priced goods, aiming for volume sales at the lower end of the consumer market, are _____ goods.

Write sentences to help you remember these expressions. Include well-known examples, e.g. *Gucci is a premium-priced up-market brand.*

19 Aggressive pricing

Read the newspaper report about SAWA, a computer games company which is introducing a new low-priced product to help win a bigger market share. Then fill each gap in the report with a phrase from the box.

~~advance orders~~   aggressive pricing   break even   factory gate price
high penetration   market share   premium price   price war
production costs   recommended retail price

SAWA in low price game

The Japanese computer games company SAWA is planning an October launch for a new game called Bird. The development of the game has taken two years but (1) _**advance orders**_ are impressive. The company expects the product to (2) _____ within one year. (3) _____ are low as the labour input in this sector is relatively small.

Margins in computer games are usually high, but SAWA has promised a (4) _____ strategy, with a competitive pricing policy. This is a change of policy for SAWA, whose products have always carried a (5) _____ , SAWA being a relatively exclusive brand. The (6) _____ is expected to be round $55, with the (7) _____ being around 33% of that. Such a low price may have the effect of creating a (8) _____ in the computer games market. (9) _____ is a new policy for SAWA, as the company aims to increase its (10) _____ in the lower end of the games market.

A further point of interest is that SAWA predict a long shelf-life for Bird, perhaps five years, which is longer than normal in this sector.

In the UK a good example of a **price war** occurred in the newspaper market, where News International published *The Times* at a much lower price than its competitors in an attempt to drive at least one of them out of the market. The strategy was not successful.

20 Pricing policy

Read the report on a meeting about pricing policy in Callan Ltd, a clothing manufacturer. Think about the meaning of the words in bold type. Then mark sentences 1–12 True or False. If a sentence is false, explain why.

Report

Subject: Marketing Focus Group Meeting

Date: 4 December 2001

Present: DF, HT, PT, JF

The following decisions were taken regarding pricing strategy for the new year.

i.   **Budget-priced goods** will only be sold in Category 'C' stores. These stores are in locations with a particular consumer profile. We expect high volume sales with low margins.

ii. Goods can only be sold at a **sale price** where they have already been offered at the **recommended retail price** for a period of not less than three months.

iii. Agents shall be instructed that from January 1, we do not allow **discounts** on any goods not sold at a previously higher price for a period of three months.

iv. Decisions on pricing must realize **margins** for the retailer of up to 25%. Margins below 15% are unlikely to be economic for any of our retailers.

v.   Similarly, our own **factory gate price** must allow the company to cover all **production costs** and also to realize a profit of between 25 and 35%. Our marketing team should watch the **market prices** to ensure that we do not price ourselves above the **going rate**.

vi. Wherever possible, we should sell our products to retailers. This will cut out intermediaries and avoid retail prices being forced higher by high **wholesale prices**.

1	Budget-priced goods are sold at a lower price than they were offered at before.	T/(F)
2	The recommended retail price is the price the manufacturer thinks a retailer should charge for a product.	T/F
3	A discount is a reduced price offered after a period on offer at a higher price.	T/F
4	The margin is the difference between the cost of a product to a manufacturer or retailer and the price the manufacturer or retailer receives when the product is sold.	T/F
5	An economic price is a price that allows a reasonable profit.	T/F
6	The factory gate price is the cost of producing the product for the factory.	T/F
7	Production costs are the expenses a manufacturer has to pay for labour.	T/F
8	The market price is the price one company charges for a product.	T/F
9	The going rate is the price the consumers are prepared to pay.	T/F
10	Retail price is the price consumers actually pay.	T/F
11	The wholesale price is the price paid by consumers who buy many examples of the same product.	T/F
12	A sale price is a special low price, reduced from an earlier price. Goods offered for sale at a sale price are often at the end of their life or the season is at an end. For example, camping equipment may be put in a sale at the end of summer.	T/F

This test contains examples of noun phrases consisting of two nouns, where the first one works like an adjective, qualifying the second, e.g. *market price*. Noun phrases like this are common in English. The next test also contains several examples.

21 Pricing strategy 1

Fill each gap in the sentences below with a phrase from the box.

---

budget-priced   demand curve   going rate   price war
retail margin   selling costs   ~~unit cost~~

---

1 The amount of money necessary to produce one individual example of a product is the ___*unit cost*___ .

2 The difference in price between what retailers pay for a product and what they sell the product at is called the _____ .

3 The total amount of money spent on all aspects of selling, including advertising, commissions and promotion, is known as the _____ .

4 A period during which several competitors aggressively lower their prices in an effort to build up market share is called a

_____ .

5 Products at the lowest end of the price scale are sometimes referred to as _____ goods.

6 The price which the market will accept for a product or for services is the _____ .

7 The line on a graph which shows the relationship between prices and consumer demand is called the _____ .

Price wars can get serious.

22 Pricing strategy 2

Match the words (1–9) with the definitions (a–i).

1	break-even point	**a**	The price wholesalers and distributors pay to the producer for goods.
2	discounting	**b**	A pricing strategy based on low pricing and low unit profits.
3	factory gate price	**c**	An illegal and secret agreement between competitors to fix higher prices to boost their profits.
4	inelastic demand	**d**	The day-to-day costs of running a business.
5	overheads	**e**	Sales of a product do not change much with variations in price.
6	penetration strategy	**f**	Reducing the price of goods in return for bulk sales or to a favoured customer.
7	price sensitive buyers	**g**	A product sold at a specially low price, perhaps at a loss, in the expectation that customers will spend money on other goods where margins are high.
8	loss leader	**h**	The point in the development of a product when sales begin to exceed the investment.
9	cartel	**i**	Consumers who are very attentive to price changes and look for lower-priced items.

Drawing graphs and other figures can help you to remember new vocabulary. There are many examples in this book where a simple sketch can help explain what something means.

23 Costs

Choose the best definition for each of the words or phrases.

1 cost of labour
   a) cost of all work involved in making a product or service ready for sale
   b) cost of manual workers employed by a company
   c) cost of industrial action by employees

2 cost of production
   a) selling price for a finished product
   b) all expenses for raw materials, heating, lighting, electricity, etc.
   c) all costs involved in making a product ready for distribution and sale

3 cost of sales
   a) total costs involved in making a product or service, distributing it and selling it
   b) cost of selling a product in salaries, commissions, etc.
   c) the price of a product when it is sold

4 commission
   a) a royalty paid to an inventor of a product
   b) a percentage of the selling price which is paid to the seller, usually an agent or distributor
   c) instructions given to a sales representative or to the shop which is asked to sell a product

5 selling costs
   a) the total money raised selling a product or service
   b) the costs involved in distributing, promoting and selling a product
   c) the salaries and other expenses paid to the sales representatives

6 direct costs
   a) all costs relating to production of a product, including development costs and raw materials, electricity and labour
   b) all taxes paid to the government
   c) the cost of labour involved in making a product

7 direct labour costs
   a) all costs relating to production of a product, including development costs and raw materials, electricity and labour

b) all labour costs involved in actual production of a product

c) all labour costs involved in producing a product and, in addition, all support labour costs, such as secretarial and administrative work

8 fixed costs

a) prices established by the government

b) costs which are decided by the management of a manufacturing company, not by suppliers or retailers

c) costs which do not depend on quantity of production, e.g. heating, lighting, rent

9 variable costs

a) costs which change according to the quantity of production, such as raw materials, components, overtime pay, etc.

b) costs which are difficult to estimate as they may suddenly change because of changes in the market, such as competitors' pricing

c) costs which change according to the time of the year, e.g. warm clothes for winter, or summer fashions

10 overheads

a) regular costs associated with the day-to-day running of a company

b) additional expenses because of a higher than expected demand for products

c) extra costs above what was planned in the costs budget

11 unit cost

a) the costs associated with all production of all products

b) the costs involved in making one single example of a product

c) the total costs for any one part of a factory producing one type of product

12 labour input

a) the cost of labour in producing products for distribution and sale

b) additional payments to workers during periods of high demand

c) the costs of all non-managerial wages and salaries

24 The classic distribution channel

Fill in the spaces on the flow chart with terms from the box.

> agent   customer   distributor   haulage company
> producer   retailer   sales representative

1 *producer*

2 _____

3 _____

4 _____

5 _____

6 _____

7 _____

Classic **distribution channels** have altered in many fields. For example supermarkets and other major retailers take care of their own distribution, buying directly from producers, so the role of the traditional wholesaler as an intermediary has declined. Many producers also sell directly to their customers, reducing the role of High Street dealers. An example is Dell Computer Corporation, a market leader in business computer systems.

25 Distribution and shipping methods

A Look at the diagram and then complete the spaces in the text that follows.

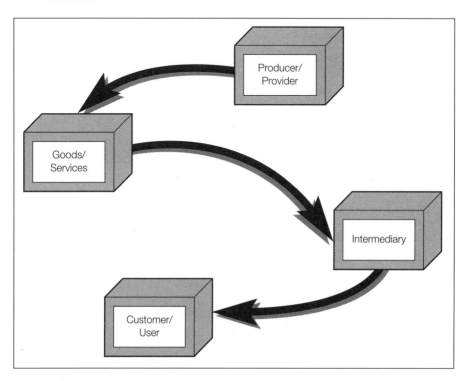

Shipping, or shipment, in the marketing or selling sense, means the despatch of (1) ___*goods*___ from the (2) _____ to the (3) _____ , or to an (4) _____ . The entire process of moving goods or (5) _____ from the producer or (6) _____ to the customer or (7) _____ is described as the (8) _____ process. It is also known as (9) _____ , one of the four Ps.

B Write the number of each picture next to the correct method of transportation.

cargo plane	_____	despatch rider	_____
delivery van	_____	freight train	_____
container ship	_____	container lorry	_____
barge	_____		

C Match the terms on the left with the descriptions on the right.

1	air freight transportation	a	a business specializing in rapid delivery of small items, usually by van or motorbike.
2	despatch rider	b	a company specializing in moving heavy goods and raw materials by train
3	shipping line	c	the business of moving large quantities of goods by air
4	courier service	d	a company specializing in transportation of goods by sea, typically using container vessels (large ships designed to transport goods) based at container ports.
5	rail freight operator	e	a company that transports goods by lorry. Major road distribution networks link so-called dry port facilities, often located near major airports and road junctions.
6	road haulage contractor	f	someone who works for a courier company delivering small items by motorbike

- The terms relating to distribution in this test mainly concern manufactured products rather than services. The exception might be the special delivery of documents, which could be undertaken by a **despatch rider** or by a **courier**. Despatch riders and courier firms specialize in rapid door-to-door delivery.

- Look for examples of companies that illustrate terms 1, 3, 4, 5 and 6. Write sentences about them, e.g. *Data Express is the courier service that my company uses.*

26 Services and the public sector

Read the text then choose the best definition – a, b or c – for each of the terms in bold.

Where the private sector leads, the public sector follows

For many years, Place, meaning distribution, was mainly associated with traditional manufactured goods and the process of transferring them from producers to consumers. Businesses had to promote their goods in a **competitive environment**, so marketing became more important. In
line 5 addition, businesses began to study their methods of distribution.

This has also happened in the service sector (banking, tourism, retailing, professional services, etc) and more recently, even in the **public sector**. The public sector has had to adapt to big changes in the business environment. There is more competition, customers are better informed
10 and better educated, and the public want better quality products and better service. **Service providers**, including local government organisations, **public health services**, schools and colleges, now find that they have to work in ways that are more similar to the private sector. They also have to be more **accountable** and less secretive.

15 This means that **public sector services**, like private and manufacturing businesses before them, have become as interested in **logistics**. The study of logistics tries to improve the systems of provision. It aims to save money and improve performance by reducing waste, so distribution has become a focus of attention. Public sector providers and
20 other service industries often deal directly with the public, or with their customers, which makes **communication skills** very important. Promotion, effective design and comfortable surroundings are part of good communication. Communication itself may be face-to-face, or it may be by post, by telephone, by email, or through websites. To sum up,
25 today the total package of the service happens in a much more complex and competitive context. The total provision includes all the physical evidence (publications, information leaflets, buildings, etc), customer support and the answering of casual enquiries, as well as the **core product** (transport, or education, or food, or any other service). The
30 public expects the best! If the service is no good, complain! If it is still no good, change your supplier – *if you can!*

1   competitive environment (line 4)
    a) a situation where businesses decide together how to divide the
       market between them
    b) a situation where businesses have to make sure they protect
       the environment
    (c) a situation where many businesses all try to get customers by
       offering the best deal or price

2   the public sector (line 7)
    a) the general public – all the people
    b) the part of the economy that is owned by central or local
       government
    c) information that is not kept secret but available to everybody

3   service providers (line 11)
    a) organizations that offer a service, not manufactured goods
    b) people who work in after-sales
    c) types of software that provide access to the Internet

4   public health services (line 12)
    a) city parks, swimming pools and sports centres
    b) hospitals, doctors' surgeries, health clinics and nursing
    c) ambulances and other transport for the sick and elderly

5   accountable (line 14)
    a) able to explain and publish details of their actions
    b) able to make enough money to stay in business even when the
       market is weak
    c) trained to keep good financial records

6   public sector services (line 15)
    a) services provided by government (local or central) such as
       health, education, road maintenance etc
    b) charities, churches and church services
    c) organizations that work throughout the whole country

7 logistics (line 16)
   a) the study of finance and accounting in business
   b) the study of using high technology equipment in business
   c) the study of systems and ways to improve efficiency

8 communication skills (line 21)
   a) the ability to convey the right messages in the best possible
      way
   b) the ability to get your message across to people in their own
      language
   c) the ability to put information into a computer system

9 core product (line 28)
   a) the fundamental thing that a business or organization provides
   b) the complete consumer experience of a business
   c) the total offering of a company or organization, including its
      advertising, buildings, staff, reputation

The public sector is also called the **state sector**. Public sector marketing is
also called **organizational marketing**, because it is organizations, not
companies, that are responsible for the services provided. Examples of such
organizations include universities, hospitals, city authorities, arts and leisure
administrations, tourist information offices, police, ambulance and fire services.

27 Electronic trading

Any business or commerce that is carried out over the Internet is electronic trading. The contact may use local telephone connections, or it may be international, and use long-distance telephone and satellite links.

A   Put each of these nine terms under the correct description.

> access code   browsing   e-business   e-commerce   ~~e-shopping~~
> home shopping   password   surfing   virtual shopping

Buying things over the Internet	Business over the Internet	A personal identification for access to a website or a security protected resource	Looking for information on the Internet
e-shopping	_____	_____	_____
_____	_____	_____	_____
_____			

B What do these abbreviations stand for?

1 EDT _____

2 EFT _____

3 ICT _____

4 ISP _____

C Match each term on the left with the correct definition on the right.

1 online support   **a** illegally accessing a company's computer systems

2 web support   **b** designing something (e.g. an Internet site) to suit the owner's needs and preferences

3 advertising on the web   **c** on the web or via the Internet

4 website   **d** extra help available over the Internet from a company's website

5 modem   **e** an Internet resource dedicated to one user, company or organization

6 homepage   **f** help or after-sales service available through the Internet

7 online   **g** personalised communication sent from one Internet user to another

8 distance learning via the web   **h** the time of day when connection charges are most expensive

9 hacking   **i** carrying out banking tasks over the Internet

10 customizing   **j** using the Internet and a website to promote products or services

11 download   **k** the time of day when connection charges are least expensive

12	peak time	l	education services offered using a website, email and other Internet support
13	off-peak	m	a company or business that specializes in doing business via the Internet
14	email	n	the opening screen on a particular website
15	e-banking	o	take information from the web or Internet and put it onto your computer
16	dot.com	p	a device that allows a computer access to telephone links and then to the Internet

The letter 'e' is now being added to a range of products and services offered electronically, for example *e-wallet*, *e-purse*. The number of e- words is growing. Expect *e-trading*, *e-finance*, *e-learning* and *e-advertising* soon and then many more!

28 Retail outlets and selling methods

Match each term in the box with a set of words in *italics* in the newspaper extract. Then write the number after the term.

chain stores	____	cold calling	____
commission	____	door-to-door selling	____
e-commerce	____	franchises	____
hypermarkets	____	Internet service providers (ISPs)	____
large multiples	____	mail order	____
mail order companies	_1_	purchasing power	____
specialist retailers	____	telesales staff	____
warehouses	____		

(1) *Companies which specialize in selling goods through a catalogue* sent out through the post normally have (2) *large buildings full of goods* from where the goods are despatched. (3) *Companies which own many stores* have (4) *strength in negotiating prices* where manufacturers are concerned. Small shops do not have this. (5) *Retail outlets which pay a licence fee to trade under a famous brand name* often benefit from increased business, since the name is a powerful advertisement.

(6) *Going from one house to another, knocking on doors,* is a highly labour-intensive type of sales operation. This type of work is normally paid on the basis of a (7) *percentage of the sales achieved being paid to the seller*. Another type of selling is by (8) *a combination of catalogue and ordering by post*. This may be complemented by (9) *personnel who sell by telephone*, trained to deal with customers' calls. Another kind of telephone selling is through (10) *telephoning someone who is not expecting your call but whom you think might buy your product*. The idea is to get your prospective customer to agree to buy your products or receive a home visit for a demonstration. A variation on this – popular with banks and the financial services industry – is to call existing customers and offer them new products.

(11) *Large out-of-town stores selling a huge range of goods* have had a serious effect on business for smaller, city centre shops. (12) *Small shops offering a personalized and highly specialized service* can survive better than small shops which try to compete directly with the larger outlets and other (13) *retail outlets owned by the same company and trading under the same name.* In recent years (14) *selling over the Internet* has become much more common. Customers order and pay for goods or services by accessing a website from a home or office computer. Companies wanting to trade over the Internet need access to the world wide web (WWW) which is provided by one of the (15) *companies that provide access to the net.*

The variety of **selling techniques** has increased remarkably in recent years. Some industries, such as banking, have moved enthusiastically into **e-commerce**, completely changing the customer's experience. Many shops now offer **e-shopping** and a home delivery service (see Test 27). However, old traditions live on. Most towns and cities still have traditional street markets!

The growth in **hypermarkets**, **supermarkets**, **chain stores** and **multiples** has had a big impact on the **small business sector**. Many small **retailers** have disappeared, but some have continued to trade profitably. One way that small **specialist retailers** have survived is by forming **buying groups**, which provide them with **economies of scale** and **cost benefits** (see Test 56).

Franchises also help small businesses to compete. A parent company (the **franchisor**) grants a **licence** to use its name to a smaller business (the **franchisee**). Hypermarkets, supermarkets and railway stations increasingly have *in-plants* – smaller shops which operate within them and pay them rent – and these are often franchises. Another recent development is the growth in *convenience stores*. These are small food and grocery outlets, selling fresh milk and bread, and also newspapers, confectionery, and so on. They are often open long hours. Many are attached to petrol stations. See also Tests 30, 55, 57 and 58.

Test yourself! Take a blank piece of paper and see how many different types of retail outlet or selling methods you can remember.

29 Planning a distribution system

Replace each underlined word in the email with a word from the list below that has a similar meaning. Write the number after the word.

consumers _____ despatch _____ e-business _____

mail order _____ middlemen _____ multiples _____

producer __1__ retailers _____ sales forces _____

sales representatives _____ wholesalers _____

Date 24 Nov 2000
From: chenement@sun1.valdisere.fr
To: silver@aro.frieberg.de
Subject: Planning a distribution system

Dear Sara,

As the (1) <u>manufacturer</u>, we obviously must ensure that products reach (2) <u>customers</u> with maximum efficiency.
At present we use independent (3) <u>distributors</u>, but we should consider better alternatives. The following changes need urgent consideration:

- Cutting out (4) <u>intermediaries</u> – this would bring cost savings.
- Larger (5) <u>sales teams</u>.
- Many more (6) <u>reps</u>.
- Improved (7) <u>shipment</u> systems.
- Closer relationships with (8) <u>dealers</u>.
- More links with (9) <u>chains</u>.
- More use of (10) <u>direct selling by post</u>.
- Using our website for more (11) <u>selling over the Internet</u>.

Please call me to discuss these points as soon as possible.
Regards

Alain
Alain Chenement
Logistics Supervisor

---

30 Distribution 1

Complete each sentence below with a word or phrase from the box.

> ~~commission agents~~   copyright   franchise agreement
> independent distributors   patent   sales force   shelf space
> sole distribution agreement   vending machine

1 Agents who receive a percentage of the sales are
   __*commission agents*__ .

2 An agreement to sell only one manufacturer's goods is called a
   _____ .

3 All the people involved in selling a company's goods or services
   are the _____ .

4 People who buy from companies and sell to retailers are called
   _____ .

5 A licence registering an invention and protecting ownership is
   called a _____ .

6 The amount of space given over in a shop for displaying a
   particular product is called _____ .

7 An agreement to pay a licence fee to use a well-known name is
   called a _____ .

8 A machine in which you put coins to buy confectionery or other
   small items is called a _____ .

9 Ownership of the reproduction rights of intellectual property
   (written words, music, film, art, etc) is protected by
   _____ .

Commission agent and *franchise agreement* are both noun + noun
combinations. Sometimes the words in the noun + noun combination
become more closely linked: then they are written with a hyphen (-), e.g.
shelf-life. When they become very widely used, the hyphen often disappears
and they become one word, e.g. *website*.

31 Distribution 2

Here is an extract from a marketing consultant's report on distribution systems in the fast moving consumer goods (FMCG) sector. The report describes three distribution systems. Write the number of each description next to the correct system.

vertical marketing system (VMS)   _____

conventional marketing system (CMS)   _____

total systems approach (TSA)   _____

Distribution systems

We can identify three main distribution systems:

1 Traditionally there used to be a line consisting of independent producers, wholesalers and retailers. Each was a separate business.

2 Now, many businesses work together in a unified system where producers, wholesalers and retailers act together. They may be under common ownership, or they may have contracted to work together as a single system.

3 However, a new trend is a distribution system which is designed to accommodate consumer needs at minimum cost, and places every step of the distribution channel under a single control.

Conclusion
In reality, the benefits to consumers of a simplified distribution process may not be as great as one might have thought. However, company profits can certainly rise.

Big **retailers** increasingly use a TSA method of control. In the UK and elsewhere they have been criticized for pressurizing producers into supplying greater quantities at lower cost and not necessarily passing the benefits on to consumers. The danger for producers is that they become dependent on the massive orders from big retailers, but the retailers may drop them without warning and the producer is left without an outlet.

32 Promotion and advertising

Next to each type of promotion write the number of the correct picture.

banner towing	5
billboard	___
flyer	___
free sample	___
freebie	___
newspaper advertisement	___
offer	___
sandwich board	___
sponsorship	___
T-shirt advertising	___
TV commercial	___

1. CHOCOLATE THAT IS OUT OF THIS WORLD — PLANET

2. TONY'S HARDWARE — POWER TOOLS 20% OFF!

3. DS SERVICES 01905 831027

4. WHEAT PUFFS — WHEAT PUFFS WIN! WEEK-END IN PARIS

5. (plane towing banner)

6. SPLASH

7. SHELL / YELLO / LUX / BASKS / COLA

COUNTY FOOD FAYRE JUNE 12-15

8. LAST MINUTE BARGAINS FOR A TROPICAL PARADISE — COME TO DREAM HOLIDAYS

9. LEX — MORE THAN JUST A CAR

10. ONE DAY ONLY MASSIVE REDUCTIONS ON NEW STOCK! MORRIS BROS ELECTRICAL

11. MRS BAGGS HOME MADE CAKES — MRS BAGGS JUST LIKE GRANNY'S

33 Communication and consumers

Next to each word or phrase in the box write the number of the correct picture.

commercial	_6_	discount	_____
mailing list	_____	mass media	_____
point-of-sale advertising	_____	reply coupon	_____
slogan	_____	target audience	_____
website	_____		

1   CRYSTAL COMMUNICATION MAKES COMMUNICATION CRYSTAL CLEAR.

2   *If you buy 200, we'll cut the price by 10%.*

3

SD Financial Services
Freepost 6723, Dewsbury, Leeds LS14 6OFT UK
Tel: 44 (0)113 453 9898
Email: SDFinance@toplink.co.uk http://www.sdfs.co.uk

Yes please! Send me further details of the complete Home Finance Plan.

Name: _____
Address: _____
_____
_____
Telephone: (home) _____ (work) _____
e-mail _____

9
Araldi, V. Via Dante 38, San Giorgio a Cremano (NA)

Arcometti, P. Corso Occidentale 42, Pisa (PI)

Arione, G. Via Garibaldi 2, La Morra (CN)

Armando, Dino, Via Stretta 10, San Gimignano (FI)

Assenzi, P. Piazza della Libertà 32, Vicenza (VI)

Attametti, F. Via dei Caduti sul Lavoro 22, Trastevere, Roma

When you browse the Internet keep a pen and notebook handy to write down new words and phrases in English. The web and all forms of advertising offer opportunities to read current, real, functional examples of English in action.

34 Planning advertising

SPEAR, a mail order company, is planning a new advertising campaign. Below is an extract from an internal report to senior marketers in the company. Fill each gap in the report with a word or phrase from the box.

> advertisements   advertising mix   campaign   ~~catalogue~~
> commercials   competition   consumer awareness   direct mail
> hard sell   impulse buying   mailshot   online   website

ADVERTISING PLAN

Our plan is to sell products through a (1) __*catalogue*__ and mail order service. We will use a high pressure, (2) _____ approach. We can attract customers to order the goods by offering special (3) _____ prizes. Once the catalogue arrives, consumers will order goods which have an instant appeal. We will depend on (4) _____ .

Another approach is to run a long advertising (5) _____ to increase (6) _____ of our products. We plan a variety of advertising techniques: this (7) _____ will consist of television (8) _____ , newspaper (9) _____ , and street advertising. We have a good target customer database, so we will use (10) _____ . We plan to do a (11) _____ twice, to put extra pressure on those who do not answer the first time.

We also have a company (12) _____ where we advertise our products. Customers can also order goods (13) _____ .

 Think of one or two well-known companies. Use some of the terms in this test to describe how they promote their products.

35 Strategies 1

Match each strategy (1–9) with the correct description (a–i).

1. Advertising on the Internet
2. A promotion strategy based on getting the consumer's attention and interest, then desire for the product, then action (buying the product).
3. All forms of advertising except mass media advertising
4. Mass media advertising
5. A selling style based on identifying and meeting the customer's needs
6. Advertising for a whole sector, such as tourism or health promotion, rather than for a specific product
7. A sales-oriented selling style, using high pressure and persuasion, discounts and free services
8. A method of sales promotion which uses pressure on distributors or on retailers
9. Advertising at the point of sale

a. generic advertising
b. below-the-line promotion
c. AIDA
d. customer-oriented selling
e. push strategy
f. above-the-line promotion
g. hard sell approach
h. in-store promotion
i. on-line promotion

Above-the-line and **below-the-line** are traditional marketing terms. Do not confuse them with the expression **online**. Above-the-line advertising would include online advertising. Below-the-line means all other forms, including in-store, on packaging, leaflets, posters, vehicles, etc.

36 Strategies 2

Fill each gap in the sentences with a word or phrase from the box.

> consumers   emotional appeal   image   promotes   publicity
>   rational appeal   targets   ~~USP (unique selling proposition)~~

1 A set of characteristics that make a product different from its competitors is its _____USP_____ .

2 Any activity which increases consumer awareness of a company or its products is _____ .

3 Promotional techniques based on giving the consumer facts and technical information are concerned with _____ .

4 Promotional techniques aimed at people's fears, ambitions, feelings, likes and dislikes are concerned with
_____ .

5 Advertising _____ consumers and _____ products.

6 Companies use websites and e-commerce strategies to appeal to new consumers and to promote a state-of-the-art
_____ .

7 Mass media promotion aims to influence public perception, not only target _____ .

Promotion is everything that raises consumer awareness of a product. That includes giving interviews to the media, **logos** on vehicles and staff wearing a uniform. **Advertising** is one type of promotion. There are many kinds of advertising and most involve paying someone else (for example a newspaper or radio station) to carry your advertisement.

37 Types of promotion

Choose the correct alternative for each sentence. In one case, both/all of the alternatives are possible.

1   direct mailing / mail order / postal advertising
Sending product or service information by post to specific
individuals or companies is called _____*direct mailing*_____ .

2   personal selling / direct selling
A selling technique based on making a personal call to an
individual or company is called _____ .

3   an in-store promotion / a special offer
A promotion based on advertising in the actual shop is

_____ .

4   point-of-sale advertising / on-pack promotion
A promotion method that involves the packaging of a product,
such as including a free sample or coupons, is called

_____ .

5   sponsorship / perimeter advertising
Advertising around the playing area at sports grounds is called

_____ .

6   bargain selling / BOGOF
A promotion method for fast moving consumer goods which
involves buying one and getting one free is called

_____ .

7   online advertising / advertising on the web / Internet advertising
Promoting your activities or your company and its products or
services on the Internet is called _____ .

8   cold calling/door-to-door selling
Telephoning direct to homes or businesses to try to interest
people in your products or services is called

_____ .

38 Promoting a message

Match the definitions (1–6) with the phrases (a–f).

1 The way the company is perceived by the public.

2 What a promotion says about its subject.

3 The attempt by marketers to give a product a unique strength, or special characteristics, in the market.

4 The person who conveys the message in the advertisement.

5 The way a message is presented in an advertisement, for example through symbols, through shock, through humour.

6 The design of an advertisement, in terms of presenting a problem, providing a solution and justifying why that solution works.

a positioning

b message structure

c message format

d corporate image

e message source

f message content

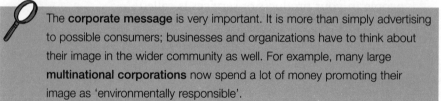

The **corporate message** is very important. It is more than simply advertising to possible consumers; businesses and organizations have to think about their image in the wider community as well. For example, many large **multinational corporations** now spend a lot of money promoting their image as 'environmentally responsible'.

39 Key words 4

Use the definitions to help you rearrange the letters to find words connected with market research.

1 A study of what people think or what they do.

yesvur _____ *survey* _____

2 A person who finds out information from the public in order to discover what they want or can afford to buy.

kemrat charseerer _____

3 A set of questions to find out people's opinions on particular issues, often used in studies of political opinion and preference.

lolp _____

4 Something that is given away free to make the customer aware of the product, or to make them try the product.

plesma _____

5 A set of questions designed to find out what people think about a product or service.

teronequinsia _____

6 Information collected from research. The researcher then analyses the information before making conclusions.

atad _____

7 Subjectivity or personal opinion affecting the results of a survey.

saib _____

8 The person who is asked questions or is studied in market research.

justceb _____

9 Another name for the person who answers questions in market research, often by returning a completed questionnaire.

pestendron _____

40 Market research objectives

A clothing manufacturer, Corallo, wants to know why its sales of jeans are falling at a rate of 10% a year. They have asked Abacus Data Research (ADR), a market research consultancy, to find out.

Choose a phrase from the box to replace each phrase in *italics* in the letter. Write the number after the phrase.

advertising research	_____	causal research study	_____
consumer awareness	_____	consumer research	_____
focus groups	_____	in-house research	_____
market research	_1_	market research brief	_____
observational research	_____	pilot questionnaire	_____
population	_____	questionnaire	_____
representative	_____	secondary research	_____

'Personally, I wouldn't be seen dead in a pair of jeans like that...'

In American English letters, it is common to use the farewell *Yours truly*. In British English letters, the standard farewell in a business letter is *Yours sincerely* when the letter starts with a name (e.g. *Dear Mr Babcock*) or *Yours faithfully* if the letter begins *Dear Sir*.

ADR
Abacus Data Research

South Dakota Blvd., Englewood Cliffs, 07632 New Jersey
Tel: 201 654 8787 Fax: 201 654 8732
email: kleins@adr.com http://www.adr.com

Sam Klein
Corallo Clothing Company
P.O. Box 230
Englewood Cliffs
May 20, 2001

Dear Sam,

Thank you for your letter dated May 15. As I said when we met briefly last week, we at ADR would be very pleased to help you with (1) *studies on your products and their markets*. What I need now is a detailed (2) *description of your objectives for this study* – a statement of exactly what you need to know.

If we set up a (3) *study that aims to explain a particular phenomenon*, in this case why you are experiencing a sales fall, we should of course go direct to consumers and ask their opinions. This type of (4) *study of what consumers think* will be vital. We can do this in three ways:

1   Using (5) *groups of typical consumers that we bring together for detailed questioning*. The members of the panel need to be (6) *typical* of the whole (7) *mass of jeans buyers*.
2   A conventional (8) *paper with a lot of questions* sent out to consumers. Alone, this is less effective, even if we use a (9) *test set of questions* to make sure we are asking the right questions. But it is much cheaper.
3   We can use (10) *studies of actual sales*. But this kind of study is based on figures, rather than on what people say, so it gives only limited information.

A further area to think about is (11) *how much consumers actually know about your company and its products*. We can carry out some (12) *studies into the effects of your advertising*.

Please send us any (13) *studies you have carried out yourselves*, or any (14) *studies using published material* that you have used in the past. This will help our background investigations.

Looking forward to hearing from you.

Yours truly,

R.McCawley

Robert R. McCawley
Deputy Vice-President

41 Types of research

Below are 11 types of market research, each followed by 4 statements.
Two of the four statements are true, and two are false. Mark the statements
T (True) or F (False).

1 agency research
a) _F_ It compares one agency with another.
b) _T_ It is carried out by independent agencies, usually experts in
particular fields.
c) _T_ It is the opposite of in-house research.
d) _F_ It is research work for governments.

2 clinical trial
a) _____ It is research carried out by clinical agencies.
b) _____ It is research into the effects of drugs or treatment methods.
c) _____ Pharmaceutical companies carry out clinical trials.
d) _____ It is a test to find out if a finished product works.

3 desk research
a) _____ It is research carried out using published material.
b) _____ It can include information about geography, politics, economics
and social conditions.
c) _____ It involves going out to ask consumers for their opinions.
d) _____ It is the study of research results using computer analysis.

4 distribution research
a) _____ It is the system of sending research material to different
consumers.
b) _____ It is about sending out information to various research
companies.
c) _____ It is research into the ways products or services are distributed.
d) _____ It is important when making decisions about where to locate
retail outlets or where agents are needed.

5 exploratory research
a) _____ It is about choosing the best research methods.
b) _____ It is designed to help marketers understand problems.
c) _____ An example of it is a detailed study of why a particular product is
losing sales.
d) _____ It is the study of new markets.

6 marketing communications research
a) _____ It is the investigation of ways to talk to consumers and the
public in general.

b) _____ It is a kind of marketing research.

c) _____ It is about the telecommunications sector.

d) _____ It looks only at the results of communication methods.

7 marketing research

a) _____ It is the same as market research.

b) _____ It is about looking at the effects of advertising.

c) _____ It includes market research.

d) _____ It is about collecting, studying and analysing information which affects marketing decisions.

8 omnibus survey

a) _____ It is research carried out on behalf of several companies together.

b) _____ It is research on the performance of many different products.

c) _____ Omnibus surveys look at several companies and compare their performance.

d) _____ It is a survey which companies can buy from the government.

9 pricing research

a) _____ It examines the relationship between price and demand.

b) _____ It is about the cost of research.

c) _____ It is very important, since price is a key element in determining market share.

d) _____ It is about profit and loss accounts.

10 primary research

a) _____ It is the first research that companies do.

b) _____ It is the most important research into a product and its market.

c) _____ It is original research carried out by a company.

d) _____ It is contrasted with secondary research, which uses published information that is easily available.

11 product research

a) _____ It looks at the market acceptance of a product.

b) _____ It involves the design and concept of a product, then testing of the product, then market acceptance of the product.

c) _____ It is about competitors' products.

d) _____ It is principally the same as quality testing.

The word research is a singular, uncountable noun. You **cannot** say *There have been a lot of researches on ...* (✗). This should be either *There has been a lot of research on ...* (✓) or *There have been a lot of studies on ...* (✓). There is also the verb *to research (something)*. The commonest expressions are *to do research* and *to carry out research*.

42 Research terms

A Match each word on the left with an appropriate word on the right to make a phrase common in market research.

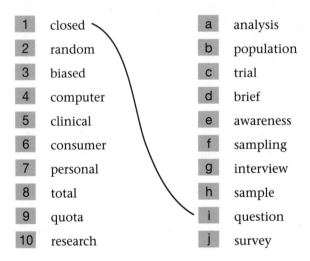

1	closed	a	analysis
2	random	b	population
3	biased	c	trial
4	computer	d	brief
5	clinical	e	awareness
6	consumer	f	sampling
7	personal	g	interview
8	total	h	sample
9	quota	i	question
10	research	j	survey

B Now match each of the phrases you have made to one of the definitions below.

1 a test carried out on a new drug

2 a survey which is not objective and has been designed to give a particular result

3 a detailed description of the objectives of some marketing research

4 a sample in which all the people taking part have been selected by chance

5 a question with a yes/no answer

6 use of ICT (Information Communications Technology) or computers to interpret results

7 what the public know about a company or product

8   choosing a sample because of the particular characteristics of the individuals

9   all the people who could possibly be consumers for a particular product

10   a survey technique based on face to face (or possibly telephone) conversation

A term that is common in market research is **socio-economic group** – a category based on occupation, education and income. Common groups are:

A   professionals: lawyers, doctors, architects, senior company executives

B   other professionals: teachers, lecturers, managers, senior police officers, senior officials

C1   higher grade officials, low grade managers, self-employed, skilled workers, shop owners, etc.

C2   semi-skilled manual workers, low grade clerical assistants, low grade civil servants

D   shop assistants, unskilled workers in regular employment

E   marginally employed and unemployed workers

Civil servants means people employed by the state, especially in government offices.

43 The research process

The picture below shows the research process, beginning with the definition of the problem, and ending with monitoring and evaluation. Study the picture, then complete the description that follows.

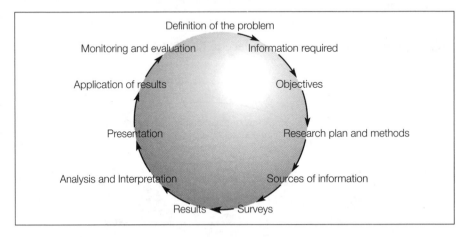

Definition of the problem

Monitoring and evaluation

Information required

Application of results

Objectives

Presentation

Research plan and methods

Analysis and Interpretation

Sources of information

Results ← Surveys

Student: Can you describe the research process?

Lecturer: Of course. The process has – according to the picture – eleven parts. Let's look at each of them in order. Well, first you have to define the problem. What is the problem? Then decide what 1) _information_ you want to find out. Next you have to set 2) _____ . The next step is to make a research plan and decide the 3) _____ of the research. After that, you have to decide where you can get the information you need, what 4) _____ . Then you have to carry out the 5) _____ , and collect 6) _____ . When you have completed this stage you must do the 7)_____ of the results and interpret the data. After that you can 8) _____ the results of the research. The research can then be applied and change can be observed. When everything is finished, you then have to 9) _____ the effects of the research, and the changes, and evaluate the whole process.

Market research is a tool to help managers make the right marketing decisions. Good marketing requires a clear **strategy**. Good research helps marketers to design good strategies. It also helps managers deal with and respond to change.

44 Research methods 1

Match the definitions (1–10) with the words and phrases (a–j).

1 Research which is designed to provide facts and statistical data. Results are easy to analyse, often by computer.

    a opinion poll

2 A sampling method based on using small groups that are representative of much larger groups.

    b validity

3 Analysis of numerical information to test that results are accurate and reliable.

    c quantitative research

4 A limited study carried out on a small number of people to test your research methods.

    d extrapolation

5 A survey designed to find out what people think, often on politics or environmental issues.

    e statistical analysis

6 A set of questions in which the answers given affect what question(s) will be asked next.

    f pilot survey

7 An original study carried out among the population, not by finding out information from published sources.

    g fieldwork

8 An essential quality for research. Without it, the research is not reliable.

    h unstructured survey

9 Using information gained from a small number of people to estimate how large numbers of (similar) people would behave in similar circumstances.

    i qualitative research

10 Research which is open-ended and gives respondents the chance to express opinions, feelings and attitudes.

    j cluster sampling

45 Research methods 2

Fill in the crossword. All the answers are terms used in research methods.

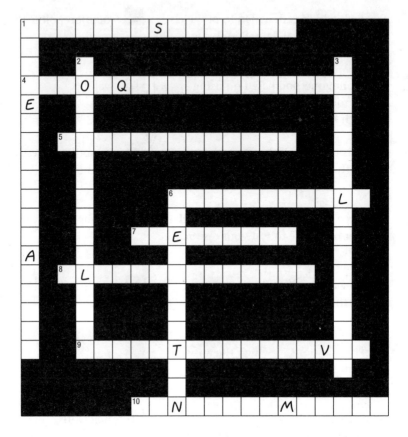

Across

1 A sampling method based on using small groups that are representative of much larger groups. (7, 8)

4 A test set of questions used on a small sample of people. It helps to identify problems in survey design. (5, 13)

5 A method of choosing who to use as research respondents that is based on identifying people with certain characteristics, e.g. males aged 18–25 who drive and have above average income. (5, 8)

6   A survey designed to find out what people think – often on political issues. (7, 4)

7   Original study carried out by going out among the population to watch people, ask questions, etc. This contrasts with finding out information from published sources such as books or reports. (9)

8   A question with a limited number of possible answers, e.g. Yes or No. (6, 8)

9   A formal design for a questionnaire which is not dependent on the answers given. (10, 6)

10   A method of selecting who will be included in a sample which ensures that the sample is representative of the whole population. (6, 8)

Down

1   A study of rival companies and their products. (10, 8)

2   A study of data using information technology hardware and software. (8, 8)

3   Questioning people individually, usually face-to-face. (8, 9)

6   A type of question which allows the person answering to use his or her own words, e.g. What do you think about Fresho Soap products? (4, 8)

Open questioning is often used in evaluation surveys. Open questioning invites respondents to say more in answer to a question. This is called **qualitative research**. It contrasts with **quantitative research**, which uses closed questions, or tick boxes. This kind of research gives results which are easily analysed, perhaps using statistical or computer analysis.
Organizations often choose a combination of qualitative and quantitative **research methods**.

46 Survey results

Look at these statistics collected from a survey. Then read statements 1–8 and mark them T (True) or F (False). If you choose False, say why.

Method: Telephone

Age:		15	16	17	18	19	20
Social group:	A	3	9	12	14	12	12
(% of age	B	23	41	26	34	25	22
group)	C1	49	20	29	35	32	38
	C2	14	10	19	10	18	16
	D	6	12	6	2	10	4
	E	5	8	8	5	3	8

1 Is eating healthy food important for you?

(% of total)	Yes	7	19	5	8	27	6
	No	4	5	3	2	12	2

2 How often do you eat healthy food?

	15	16	17	18	19	20
Always	1	2	–	–	3	–
Most of the time	2	3	6	1	2	1
Sometimes	4	2	1	–	11	1
Rarely	1	3	1	7	14	2
Never	3	14	–	2	9	4

1 The survey shows the young prefer healthy food. Ⓣ/F

2 The survey was based on telephone interviews. T/F

3 The respondents were aged 14–19. T/F

4 The majority (72%) thought that eating healthy food was 'important' for them. T/F

5 25% said that 'most of the time' they ate 'reasonably healthy food'. T/F

6 Higher status groups were clearly more interested in healthy eating. T/F

7 It was not possible to draw firm conclusions about the relationship between age and healthy eating, as there is no consistent trend in the results. T/F

8 The survey is biased since most of the respondents were in higher socio-economic groups. T/F

47 Key words 5

A Find eight common words connected with consumers and market segmentation in the word square. Three of the words are vertical, and five are horizontal.

P	O	S	I	T	I	O	N	I	N	G
P	B	E	K	L	M	O	G	R	G	F
O	N	G	L	D	Q	U	I	R	T	G
I	G	M	R	B	C	D	L	B	A	E
N	B	E	H	A	V	I	O	U	R	R
G	E	N	D	I	F	F	Y	N	G	D
A	E	T	H	I	C	S	A	I	E	L
N	M	G	E	L	S	P	L	M	T	E
U	S	L	I	F	E	S	T	Y	L	E
L	O	Y	M	E	N	T	Y	T	U	C
A	T	T	I	T	U	D	E	N	S	E

B Match the terms you have found in the word square with the meanings below.

1 The way people live, work and spend their leisure time.

2 The special orientation of a product towards a particular target group of consumers.

3 A part of the overall market.

4 The tendency for consumers to stay with one product or one producer, and not to use similar ones from competitors.

5 What a consumer feels or thinks.

6 Considerations based on moral questions and moral judgements.

7 What consumers actually do.

8 Particular consumers at whom a producer directs promotional effort.

48 Consumer marketing and buyer behaviour

A Match the term on the left with the definition on the right.

1 marketing ethics

a An established liking for a particular producer's products that means you often buy the same product again, even over many years.

2 niche marketing

b Large purchases of products that will be used for a long time, even for years. Such purchases are often thought about a lot, with a high level of customer involvement.

3 brand loyalty

c A spontaneous decision to buy something – you see it – you buy it!

4 routine purchasing

d Aiming a high price, high quality product at a narrow group of consumers, with a lot of purchasing power (a lot of money!)

5 impulse buying

e Repeat buying, with little involvement in the purchase.

6 fast moving consumer goods (FCMG)

f Regularly used items that are bought frequently with little personal involvement.

7 consumer durables

g Concern for the environment, for society and for a moral code in marketing.

B Fill each gap in the sentences below with a preposition from the box. The prepositions may be used more than once.

> at   in   into   of   on   to   with   for   about

1 People who are concerned __*about*__ society are typically interested _____ marketing ethics.

2 Niche marketing is frequently concerned _____ aiming particular products _____ specific socio-economic groups.

3 Brand loyalty is based _____ the development _____ routine purchasing of low-involvement goods.

4 The success of shops attached _____ petrol stations depends _____ impulse purchasing. You can see motorists who suddenly decide to buy a music cassette, confectionery or a magazine.

5 Research _____ buyer behaviour shows that when consumers make routine purchases _____ regularly used consumer products, they are not personally involved _____ the products.

6 Routine purchasing contrasts _____ the purchase of consumer durables, such as furniture, kitchen appliances or a car. Here there is a greater degree _____ personal involvement.

7 Clients have increasingly high expectations _____ the providers of professional services in a range of fields, including health, education and the law.

8 Special government appointed committees are responsible _____ ensuring that consumers get good service and adequate protection. Sometimes called consumer watchdogs, they respond _____ reports of malpractice.

Check that you know the meaning of these terms: **niche marketing, routine purchasing, (brand) loyalty, impulse purchasing, (marketing) ethics, consumer durables**. If they are new to you, practise using them by writing sentences about yourself and your **buyer behaviour**.

49 Economic factors and buyer behaviour

Fill each gap in the text below with a word or phrase from the box. The items in **bold** are headings.

assets	**credit availability**	discounts	discretionary income
economic growth	employment	~~general economic situation~~	
loss leader	outgoings	**price**	**purchasing power**

There are four major economic factors which affect consumer buying behaviour.

1 *general economic situation*

When the national economy is doing well, when people feel that their _____ is safe, they spend more. In times of a slow down in _____ , if interest rates or taxation rates increase, then buyer confidence goes down.

2 _____

People spend according to what is left after meeting their regular costs on rent, mortgage, bills, tax, borrowings and other _____ . What is left is called _____ .

3 _____

Banks and other lenders are sometimes particularly happy to lend, for example to anyone in work, or with _____ such as property. Credit card spending goes up and many people borrow money to buy goods.

4 _____

This is perhaps obvious. High prices may limit spending, but not always. Sometimes high prices indicate high quality and this increases the desirability of the product. Price may also be less important if the need is great. But, in contrast, low prices may increase buying, especially where _____ are on offer. Sometimes items are offered at a low price as a _____ . This means products are sold at below cost price. The shop thinks that consumers will buy these low priced goods, but also other high profit items.

I just came in for some tea bags and a chicken curry, but I think I'll have this entertainment centre instead.

Supermarkets often sell some regularly purchased **fast moving consumer goods** (FMCGs) at below **cost price** as part of a **loss leader strategy**. Special offers on the other hand are often to introduce a new product or to boost sales of a particular item. Special offers are usually temporary, but a loss leader strategy can be a long-term decision for some items. In both cases, the supermarket is predicting **consumer behaviour/buyer behaviour**.

50 Consumers and lifestyle

Match the consumer type (1–8) to the lifestyle definitions (a–h).

1	achiever	**a**	This person has a traditional, conservative and conformist lifestyle. He or she likes to feel comfortable but does not like change.
2	belonger	**b**	This person has the original idea to do something.
3	decision maker	**c**	This person is young, ambitious, successful, hard-working and determined to win in life.
4	dependent	**d**	This person is ambitious and competitive, and seeks to become richer and more successful, but is content with life.
5	emulator	**e**	This person has worked hard and got what he or she wanted. He/she is rational and reasonable.
6	influencer	**f**	This person announces that something is going to happen.
7	initiator	**g**	This person tells other people about an innovation they think is a good one, and recommends buying.
8	integrated	**h**	This person is unable to survive well alone because of age, lack of money or a physical or mental disability.

When marketers talk about **prospects** they mean potential buyers of a product. A key aim of **promotion** is to persuade prospects to become **purchasers**. **Market segmentation** aims to categorize prospects, usually by **lifestyle** and **spending power**.

51 Market segmentation 1

Mark statements 1–8 T (True) or F (False). If a statement is false, correct it.

1   *Social marketing* targets particular consumers according to their socio-economic group.   T / F

2   *Target marketing* is concerned with advertising to particular groups of consumers.   T / F

3   *Differentiated marketing* aims to appeal to specifically identified groups of potential users of a product.   T / F

4   *Undifferentiated marketing* is all kinds of marketing techniques used at once.   T / F

5   *Segmentation strategy* is an attempt to divide the total market into specific types of consumers.   T / F

6   *Product positioning* is a way of promoting goods in stores.   T / F

7   *Industrial marketing* is the marketing of manufactured goods.   T / F

8   *Consumer watchdogs* have become more common especially in service industries and in public sector.   T / F

On socio-economic groups, see Test 42. On industrial marketing, see Test 53.

52 Market segmentation 2

Complete the table below by writing the words and phrases from the next page under the right heading.

Types of market segmentation		
Behaviouristic segmentation	**Benefits segmentation**	**Demographic segmentation**
use/non-use of product	product characteristics	age
Geographic segmentation	**Industrial market segmentation**	**Psychographic segmentation**
state/country	turnover	opinions

climate

~~product characteristics~~

ethnic origin

size of company

nationality

region

political beliefs

~~opinions~~

~~use/non use of product~~

~~turnover~~

leisure interests

urban/suburban/rural

~~age~~

knowledge/awareness of a product

attitudes to a product

~~state/country~~

type of company

sex

product performance

53 Industrial marketing

Industrial marketing is marketing by companies where the target audience is another company, or organization, not individual consumers or members of the public. Completely different marketing strategies are involved.

A Read the extract from a management training book below. Fill in the gaps with headings from the box.

> buyer factors   external factors   needs
> price and promotional factors   supplier factors

Influences on industrial purchasing

Industrial marketers must understand what affects buying decisions in companies and organizations. Then they can plan a marketing strategy. We can say that buying is affected by five factors.

1 _____ , for example discounts, special prices and terms, as well as the influence of advertising, free samples, and trial offers.

2 _____ , or what people say about the company, exhibitions and trade fairs, reviews and comments in trade journals, and also any relevant seasonal factors.

3 _____ . Examples are the buyer's experience, and knowledge of the product, and of the potential suppliers. The culture of the buying organization is also important, and an understanding of the company purchasing policy. The size, complexity, level of technology, and financial resources are all important. A final factor in this category is the structure of the organization, and the role of senior executives in buying decisions.

4 _____ including level of urgency, stock levels, and the perceived value of the purchase to the buying organization.

5 _____ include competitors and rival offers, the quality and availability of the product offered, after-sales service, location and labour relations at the suppliers. Another significant factor here is the relationship with existing suppliers, including personal relationships, and the desire for continuity.

B Find words in the text above which go with these definitions. They are in the right order.

1 Special reduced prices

2 Conditions attached to payment, such as dates and credit

3 Special industry events to show off products

4 Specialist magazines

5 Rules about buying goods and services

6 Quantity of equipment held in storage

7 Support provided buy a seller to a buyer

8 The relationship between a company and its employees

Industrial marketing is affected by the industry environment. Porter described **Five Forces** of the industry environment: **competition** (Who are they?) and the nature of competition (Price or quality?); new **entrants** to the market (How easy or difficult is it to enter the market?); **substitutes** (E.g. travel by plane instead of by bus); **customers** (How much power do they have? How much choice?); **suppliers** (How many suppliers are there? If there are very few, they have more power).[1]

[1] Porter M., *Competitive Strategy: Techniques for Analysing Industries and Competitors*, (New York: Free Press, 1980), p. 7

54 Key words 6

SECTION 8

A   Match each word (1–6) with its opposite (a–f).

1	overseas	**a**	free market economy
2	strength	**b**	global
3	buyers	**c**	domestic
4	supply	**d**	weakness
5	command economy	**e**	suppliers
6	local	**f**	demand

B   Now fill each gap in the sentences with a word or phrase from part A.

1   Nabisco has dominated the _____ biscuit market in the USA for over 60 years.

2   The enormous _____ of the McDonald's brand name has helped the company to enter new markets all over the world.

3   A _____ of small retail businesses is their inability to compete with larger competitors in fixing favourable terms with _____ .

4   All major European manufacturers have to look to _____ markets to increase their turnover.

5   When commercial _____ purchase large quantities of goods, it is often possible to achieve important cost savings.

6   Effective pricing policy depends on the _____ and _____ relationship.

7   The WTO, NAFTA, Japan and the EU are committed to the values of the _____ .

8   Globalization has caused many businesses to look to _____ markets and not just _____ ones.

80   Section 8: Planning and international marketing

Marketers have to think about the impact of **globalization** on their business. What exactly is globalization? Here's a definition: globalization is 'the increasing diversity, cultural impact and extent of trade, communication, political, economic and security interests, aid, investment, industrial and commercial ownership, wealth generation and environmental awareness across and between regions where distance and location are less significant than they once were'.

An example of the impact of globalization is the increase in **Foreign Direct Investment** (FDI). FDI is investment of money in another country. 'FDI jumped from around $50 billion in 1985 to $644 billion in 1998 and was on track to top $800bn in 1999' *United Nations World Investment Report* 1999 New York and Geneva, quoted in Micklethwait J. & Woodridge A. (2000, p.xxi) *A Future Perfect: the challenge and hidden promise of globalisation*, London Heinemann.

55 More key planning terms

Decide if the following terms are the same (S) or different (D). If they are different, explain how.

1. strategy / plan

2. customer/ client

3. free market / market economy

4. market trend / market survey

5. marketing mix / advertising mix

6. product mix / marketing mix

7. mission statement / corporate mission

8. opportunities / threats

9. royalty / franchise agreement

10. state sector / public sector

11. service industries / tertiary sector

12. accounting / accountability

Corporate strategy[1]

Mission statement or vision	What business are we in?
Corporate objectives, goals and aims	Where do we want to go and how do we get there?
Market research	Who are our customers? What are their needs?
Audit of external environment	What are the opportunities and threats that we face?
Analysis of resources	What are our strengths and weaknesses?
Marketing objectives	How do we achieve our objectives in marketing terms?
Strategic plan	How do we match our objectives with our resources?
Action plan	What do we have to do to achieve our objectives?

[1] Hannagan T., *Management: Concepts and Practices*, 2nd edition (London: Financial Times/Pitman Publishing, 1998), p. 125

56 Marketing planning

Fill each gap in the sentences below with a word or phrase from the box.

> accountability   competition   ~~economies of scale~~
> economies of scope   external audit   marketing audit
> marketing planning   marketing research   public sector   service

1 Increasing production by 25% does not increase costs by much, because we are able to take advantage of **_economies of scale_** .

2 A complete _____ will demonstrate all aspects of our performance in terms of meeting our marketing objectives.

3 _____ is essential to prepare clear objectives and a strategy for reaching our objectives.

4 The _____ examines factors which are not under the company's control.

5 By having documentation which can be used in various markets we are able to take advantage of _____ .

6 We are conducting _____ to try to improve all aspects of our company performance.

7 We know that marketing planning has a long history in the private sector and in manufacturing. Recently there has been a new emphasis on planning in the _____ and in all kinds of _____ industries.

8 Public sector marketing has had to respond to increased _____ and the need for _____ in all areas of service provision.

Marketing and marketing planning have become more important for **public sector service providers** and **organizations**. This is true in health, education, transport, and government-run departments. There are different reasons for this: there is more competition, governments want value for money from their departments and from their staff, the public are better informed and want better standards. See also Test 26.

57 The international trading environment

Choose the correct term for each of the definitions.

1 The market consisting of the country where a company is based and no other countries.
a) servant market
b) domestic market ⟵
c) local market

2 Factors which i) may have a negative affect on company performance, but which ii) are outside the company's control and iii) are identified during an analysis of marketing performance and prospects.
a) weaknesses
b) threats
c) quotas

3 A contract which allows another company to make your product and states the terms of payment.
a) franchise
b) a patent
c) a licence agreement

4 The action of making illegal duplicates of copyright material.
a) black market
b) cloning
c) copyright infringement

5 A large company with subsidiaries in many different countries.
a) a multinational
b) a holding company
c) a corporation

6   Factors which i) probably have a negative affect on company performance, ii) are within the company's control, and iii) are identified during an analysis of marketing performance and prospects.
a) weaknesses
b) threats
c) failures

7   A body which negotiates and then monitors international trade agreements.
a) World Trade Organisation (WTO)
b) General Agreement on Tariffs and Trade (GATT)
c) World Bank.

8   Companies which advertise and trade internationally using their own website on the Internet
a) high tech companies
b) dot.com companies
c) Internet Service Providers (ISPs)

9   Cash incentives provided by a government to encourage a company to do business overseas
a) export taxes
b) export tariffs
c) export subsidies

- The **WTO** replaced GATT in 1995. In May 2001 the WTO had 141 member countries.

- Think about how the export of services, and the international dimension to the services sector, has increased in recent years. First list the main service industries. Then write down ways in which they have become more international.

58 International marketing

Read this extract from a marketing consultant's report on options for Apsa, a Spanish food distribution company planning to expand into an international market. Then fill in the missing information on the next page.

Central/South American expansion: Options and recommendations

International marketing is a major step beyond simple *exporting*. Exporting remains essentially focused on the home producer. International marketing, in contrast, establishes a genuine presence in new markets and involves major *capital investment*.

APSA's marketing strategy in seeking to expand in Central and South America involves four options:

1. **International marketing strategy**: setting up manufacturing and sales subsidiaries. This offers the opportunity for full integration in the target market. However establishing subsidiaries is of course very capital intensive, and can be risky unless a lot of preliminary market research is done. Research must include finding out about the economy, local habits and customs, as well as about the markets for the products. This would be appropriate for Argentina, where establishing a subsidiary may be the best option. With this kind of international marketing, the subsidiaries should operate as independent cost centres with local management.

2. A second option is **franchising, or other joint ventures or partnerships** with established players in the market. This is usually less capital intensive and is probably best for Peru and Bolivia. Another advantage is that franchising is common in the food and drinks industry. With franchising individuals pay to use the name of a well-known manufacturer. The franchisor can insist on various policies, standards and purchasing practices, as well as receiving license payments and other fees from the franchisees.

3. A compromise, some way short of international marketing, is to use **overseas agents and distributors**. This is closer to a simple exporting strategy than international marketing, but it can be effective, and is definitely much cheaper. We recommend this option in Mexico and Chile. A possible problem is conflict of interest where an agent also handles a competitor's products. We suggest Apsa should try to obtain sole distribution agreements for these countries.

4. The fourth option is to abandon plans for international marketing and keep a simple **export strategy**, using direct links between APSA and customers. We do not recommend this as growth potential is very low.

Countries: **Mexico and Chile**

Preferred expansion method: _____

_____

Advantages: _____

_____

Possible difficulties: _____

_____

Recommendations: _____

_____

Countries: **Peru and Bolivia**

Preferred expansion method: _____

_____

Advantages: _____

_____

Sources of income: _____

_____

Countries: **Argentina**

Preferred expansion method: _____

_____

Advantages: _____

_____

Main disadvantages: _____

_____

Recommendations: _____

_____

- The test includes the adjective *risky*. Note the noun *risk* and the verb *to risk (something)*. There are also two common verb phrases *to run the risk of (+ ing)* and *to take a risk (in + ing)*.

  Examples: *We run the risk of legal action if we copy another company's products.*

  We should not risk it. It's too risky.

  We took a risk in setting up a plant in Rotoronga, but we made money.

  There's still a risk of political instability in Rotoronga.

- The term *purchasing practice* means how things are done. It is more common in the plural, *purchasing practices*. Note the similar phrase *common practice*, e.g. *It is common practice in most companies to have a marketing department.*

59 Growth-Share Matrix

Read the extract from a training seminar on the Growth-Share Matrix and study the diagram. Then mark statements 1–10 T (True) or F (False). If they are false, explain why.

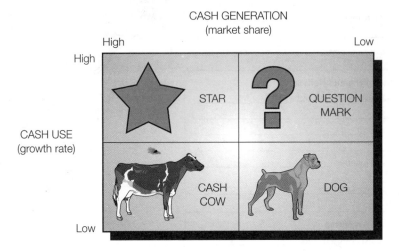

CASH GENERATION
(market share)

The Growth-Share Matrix

The Growth-Share Matrix was originally conceived by the Boston Consulting Group. It is basically a planning tool to help marketers decide which products need extra support – in terms of cash investment – and which should be dropped completely.

Cash Cows are the dream product: they generate high income but don't actually require
5 | a lot of spending. A Cash Cow product practically markets itself. A Star, on the other hand, is a new product, it requires a lot of cash, the advertising budget is high. You hope it might become a Cash Cow, but for now it offers a possibly very high short-term profit.

Question Marks, also known as Problem Products, probably need a lot of cash investment to turn them into Stars. On the other hand, they may never be really successful.
10 | At least the choice is usually clearer with Dogs: they don't use much cash, but they don't generate much income, either; they can probably be dropped.

A related concept to the Growth-Share Matrix is the idea of a Strategic Business Unit (SBU). This is the idea of treating each product area as an individual cost centre, and then being able to assess whether it is profitable or not. Profitable products – or product areas –
15 | are clearly identified as profitable, but weak and unprofitable ones are shown to be weak. With this information, it is easier to make decisions on whether to promote a weak product area using different and better marketing, or whether it would be better to drop it. If a failing product is dropped, then resources can be moved to other areas, or to develop new opportunities.

1   Cash Cows make a lot of money.   (T)/F

2   Products shown to be Dogs in the growth-share
    matrix usually need a lot of money spending on
    them. Perhaps they are not worth it.   T/F

3   Stars can make good short-term profits even though
    they use a lot of cash.   T/F

4   The Growth-Share Matrix is a planning tool designed
    to show which products need extra marketing support
    and which should be abandoned.   T/F

5   Question Marks are also known as Problem Products.   T/F

6   Companies need to make a decision on what to do
    with Question Marks – they might develop into Stars
    if given extra support.   T/F

7   SBU stands for Standard Business Unit.   T/F

8   The SBU is a tool used to identify strong and weak
    products – or product areas – in a company's product
    portfolio.   T/F

9   The SBU approach treats whole companies as a separate
    item, and highlights profit or loss.   T/F

10 The SBU approach only works in manufacturing
    industries.   T/F

60 Marketing audit

Read this email from a director of a financial services company to a colleague in an overseas subsidiary. Then fill each gap with a word or phrase from the box.

~~domestic~~	export	external audit	internal audit
marketing audit	SWOT analysis	threat	trend

Date 22 Jan 2000 15:48:45 +0900
From: J.A.W. Financial Services PLC JAWS@arena.com
To: 'Isabelle Braque' Isabraque@threecolours.com
Subject: Re. Update/news

Hello Isabelle,

Just a short note to bring you up to date while you are away. Since there has been a decline in our (1) _____ *domestic* _____ sales we have decided to carry out a (2) _____ to identify areas where improvement can be made. This consists of a typical (3) _____ with an (4) _____ to look at factors within the company and an (5) _____ examining factors outside our immediate control.

We expect that the major (6) _____ to improved performance in our domestic markets is the weakness of the national economy. The good news is that while home sales have fallen, our (7) _____ performance has been good. The (8) _____ in our key international markets is positive.

Please call me when you return to the office to discuss this in more detail.

Cheers,
John

Remember! Marketing is everybody's business

Answers

Test 1

1	product	8	producing
2	place	9	developing
3	time	10	product
4	needs	11	service
5	profit	12	price
6	customers	13	promote
7	want	14	distribute

Test 2

A

```
R Q A I J K L M P L A N
C U S T O M E R S P O Q
A A S M A R K E T I N G
H L D L F G H J T S T O
O I E E F W R U U C V O
J T M A G Y B B C E A D
L Y A T H I R U B D U S
N Q N P R O D U C T Q P
O S D T T R V G H J W R
O M S E R V I C E S X E
D I K I R E S E A R C H
D X X A P Q U A N A F H
```

B

1	quality	7	distribution
2	research	8	marketing
3	customers	9	plan
4	goods	10	mix
5	services	11	demand
6	product		

C

1	consumers	5	demand
2	customers	6	distribution
3	marketers	7	mix
4	research		

Test 3

A

1 market   marketer
   market, marketing
2 distribute   distributor
   distribution
3 compete   competitor
   competition
4 advertise   advertiser
   advertising, advertisement
5 supply   supplier
   supply
6 sponsor   sponsor
   sponsorship
7 consume   consumer
   consumption
8 produce   producer
   product, production
9 analyse   analyst
   analysis
10 research   researcher
   research
11 import   importer
   import/s

B

1 market/products
2 advertise/consumers
3 analyse/suppliers/consumers
4 import
5 supply
6 competition
7 sponsorship/advertising

Test 4

A

1	c	5	b	9	b
2	a	6	c	10	b
3	c	7	a	11	c
4	b	8	a	12	a

B

1 market leader (or market share)
2 campaign
3 market share
4 sponsorship
5 distribution (or shipment)

Test 5

1	Product	5	People
2	Price	6	Packaging
3	Place	7	Physical evidence
4	Promotion	8	Process

Test 6
1 plan
2 strengths
3 weaknesses
4 opportunities
5 threats
6 mix
7 product
8 price
9 place
10 promotion
11 process
12 people
13 physical evidence
(7–13 in any order)

Test 7
f	e	d
h	g	i
b	a	c

Test 8
1 goods	5 mix
2 free	6 plan
3 research	7 trends
4 demand	8 analysis

Test 9
1 c
2 a
3 b
4 b
5 c
6 a
7 b

Test 10
A
1 brand identity
2 brand name
3 brand image
4 own-brand
5 brand valuation
6 unbranded
7 intangible assets
8 brand loyalty
9 premium brand

B
1 brand name
2 brand valuation
3 unbranded
4 brand image
5 own-brand
6 intangible assets
7 brand loyalty
8 premium brand
9 brand identity

Test 11
augmented product 7e
clone 5c
consumer durable 2d
core product 9f
fast moving consumer goods 8b
generic product 1g
perishables 3a
primary manufacturing 4j
sell-by date 10i
service 6h

Test 12
5 Our R & D department designed the Triple X Pathway over a five-year period ...
4 ... and the product was finally launched this year.
6 The core product is, of course, a personal computer ...
2 ... but the augmented package includes ten types of software, a DVD drive, speakers, a printer, a scanner, manuals, free internet access, a free on-site warranty and the prestige of the Triple X brand name.
8 Of course, all components used in the manufacture of the Triple X Pathway have been well tested.
9 We offer a full after-sales service ...
1 ... and an extended five-year warranty with absolute confidence.
7 Furthermore, we expect the product to experience rapid early sales for at least three years ...
3 ... before being joined by me-too products from our competitors.

Test 13

A

1 development
2 launch
3 growth
4 maturity
5 saturation
6 decline

B

1 potential
2 portfolio
3 positioning
4 return
5 penetration, consumers
6 extend
7 development, quality, appeal
8 markets
9 research, decision-making

Test 14

1 launched
2 parts/labour
3 labour/parts
4 warranty
5 state-of-the-art
6 after-sales
7 network
8 customer
9 helpline
10 premium
11 on-site
12 support

Test 15

1 consumer
2 perishable
3 products
4 durables
5 added
6 retailer
7 service
8 purchased
9 patent
10 flop

Test 16

1 off
2 by
3 away
4 back
5 on
6 on
7 to
8 into

Test 17

A

A	P	R	I	C	E	L	T
D	I	S	C	O	U	N	T
E	C	R	G	S	N	O	I
M	P	O	R	T	E	V	F
A	W	R	M	S	V	I	O
N	I	P	F	E	E	O	R
D	R	L	M	H	R	G	P
A	M	A	R	G	I	N	E

B

1 profit
2 revenue
3 margin
4 price
5 discount
6 fee
7 demand
8 costs

Test 18

A

1 e
2 c
3 d
4 b
5 a

B

1 a
2 d
3 b
4 e
5 c

C

1 elastic demand
2 penetration strategy
3 premium-priced
4 fixed costs
5 budget-priced

Test 19

1 advance orders
2 break even
3 Production costs
4 high penetration
5 premium price
6 recommended retail price
7 factory gate price
8 price war
9 Aggressive pricing
10 market share

Test 20

1 False. Budget-priced means low-priced, not at a reduced price.
2 True

3 False. A discount is a specially reduced price, usually for a particular customer. A discount may be offered to a frequent customer, or if he/she buys several products.
4 True
5 True
6 False. The factory gate price is the price a manufacturer asks when selling a product to a wholesaler, agent or retailer.
7 False. Production costs are all the expenses a manufacturer has to pay to produce a product, including labour.
8 False. The market price is the typical price that different companies are asking for similar products.
9 True
10 True
11 False. The wholesale price is the price a retailer pays a wholesaler for a product.
12 True

Test 21
1 unit cost
2 retail margin
3 selling costs
4 price war
5 budget-priced
6 going rate
7 demand curve

Test 22
1 h	4 e	7 i
2 f	5 d	8 g
3 a	6 b	9 c

Test 23
1 a	5 b	9 a
2 c	6 a	10 a
3 a	7 b	11 b
4 b	8 c	12 a

Test 24
1 producer
2 haulage company
3 distributor
4 agent
5 sales representative
6 retailer
7 customer

Test 25
A
1 goods	6 provider
2 producer	7 user
3 customer	8 distribution
4 intermediary	9 Place
5 services	

B
1 despatch rider	5 barge
2 container lorry	6 container ship
3 delivery van	7 cargo plane
4 freight train	

C
| 1 c | 3 d | 5 b |
| 2 f | 4 a | 6 e |

Test 26
1 c	4 b	7 c
2 b	5 a	8 a
3 a	6 a	9 a

Test 27
A

Buying things over the Internet	Business over the Internet	A personal identification for access to a website or a security protected resource	Looking for information on the Internet
virtual shopping home shopping e-shopping	e-commerce e-business	access code password	surfing browsing

B
1 EDT Electronic Data Transfer
2 EFT Electronic Funds Transfer
3 ICT Information Communications Technology
4 ISP Internet Service Provider

C

1 f	5 p	9 a	13 k
2 d	6 n	10 b	14 g
3 j	7 c	11 o	15 i
4 e	8 l	12 h	16 m

Test 28
chain stores 13
cold-calling 10
commission 7
door-to-door selling 6
e-commerce 14
franchises 5
hypermarkets 11
internet service providers (ISPs) 15
large multiples 3
mail order 8
mail order companies 1
purchasing power 4
specialist retailers 12
telesales staff 9
warehouses 2

Test 29
consumers 2
despatch 7
e-business 11
mail order 10
middlemen 4
multiples 9
producer 1
retailers 8
sales forces 5
sales representatives 6
wholesalers 3

Test 30
1 commission agent
2 sole distribution agreement
3 sales force
4 independent distributor
5 patent
6 shelf space
7 franchise agreement

8 vending machine
9 copyright

Test 31
1 conventional marketing system (CMS)
2 vertical marketing system (VMS)
3 total systems approach (TSA)

Test 32
banner towing 5
billboard 9
flyer 10
free sample 11
freebie 3
newspaper advertisement 8
offer 4
sandwich board 2
sponsorship 7
T-shirt advertising 6
TV commercial 1

Test 33
commercial 6
discount 2
mailing list 9
mass media 5
point-of-sale advertising 7
reply coupon 3
slogan 1
target audience 8
website 4

Test 34
1 catalogue
2 hard sell
3 competition
4 impulse buying
5 campaign
6 consumer awareness
7 advertising mix
8 commercials
9 advertisements
10 direct mail
11 mailshot
12 website
13 online

Test 35

1	i	4	f	7	g
2	c	5	d	8	e
3	b	6	a	9	h

Test 36

1. unique selling proposition
2. publicity
3. rational appeal
4. emotional appeal
5. targets, promotes
6. image
7. consumers

Test 37

1. direct mailing
2. direct selling
3. an in-store promotion
4. on-pack promotion
5. perimeter advertising
6. BOGOF(Buy one get one free)
7. online advertising / advertising on the web / Internet advertising (all are possible)
8. cold calling

Test 38

1	d	3	a	5	c
2	f	4	e	6	b

Test 39

1. survey
2. market researcher
3. poll
4. sample
5. questionnaire
6. data
7. bias
8. subject
9. respondent

Test 40

advertising research 12
causal research study 3
consumer awareness 11
consumer research 4
focus groups 5
in-house research 13
market research 1
market research brief 2
observational research 10
pilot questionnaire 9
population 7
questionnaire 8
representative 6
secondary research 14

Test 41

1. a) F, b) T, c) T, d) F
2. a) F, b) T, c) T, d) F
3. a) T, b) T, c) F, d) F
4. a) F, b) F, c) T, d) T
5. a) F, b) T, c) T, d) F
6. a) T, b) T, c) F, d) F
7. a) F, b) F, c) T, d) T
8. a) T, b) T, c) F, d) F
9. a) T, b) F, c) T, d) F
10. a) F, b) F, c) T, d) T
11. a) T, b) T, c) F, d) F

Test 42

A

1	i	5	c	9	f
2	h	6	e	10	d
3	j	7	g		
4	a	8	b		

B

1. clinical trial
2. biased survey
3. research brief
4. random sample
5. closed question
6. computer analysis
7. consumer awareness
8. quota sampling
9. total population
10. personal interview

Test 43

1	information	6	results
2	objectives	7	analysis
3	methods	8	present
4	sources	9	monitor
5	surveys		

Test 44

1	c	5	a	9	d
2	j	6	h	10	i
3	e	7	g		
4	f	8	b		

Test 45

Across

1 cluster sampling
4 pilot questionnaire
5 quota sampling
6 opinion poll
7 fieldwork
8 closed question
9 structured survey
10 random sampling

Down

1 competitor analysis
2 computer analysis
3 personal interview
6 open question

Test 46

1 T
2 T
3 F The respondents were aged 15–20
4 T
5 F 15% claimed to eat reasonably healthy foods most of the time. 6% said they always ate healthy foods.
6 F This is not clear from the results
7 T
8 T

Test 47

```
P O S I T I O N I N G
P B E K L M O G R G F
O N G L D Q U I R T G
I G M R B C D L B A E
N B E H A V I O U R R
G E N D I F F Y N G D
A E T H I C S A I E L
N M G E L S P L M T E
U S L I F E S T Y L E
L O Y M E N T Y T U C
A T T I T U D E N S E
```

B

1	lifestyle	5	attitude
2	positioning	6	ethics
3	segment	7	behaviour
4	loyalty	8	target

Test 48

A

1	g	5	c
2	d	6	f
3	a	7	b
4	e		

B

1	about, in	5	into, of, in
2	with, at	6	with, of
3	on, of	7	of
4	to, on	8	for, to

Test 49

1 general economic situation, employment, economic growth
2 purchasing power, outgoings, discretionary income
3 credit availability, assets
4 price, discounts, loss leader

Test 50

1	c	5	d
2	a	6	g
3	f	7	b
4	h	8	e

Test 51

1 False. Social marketing takes general attitudes in society into account in all marketing decisions, e.g. cruelty to animals is wrong, the environment has to be protected, women should look after the children.
2 False. Target marketing is concerned with making sure a product is appropriate for specifically identified needs.
3 True
4 False. Undifferentiated marketing is aimed at everyone in society. It promotes a product and its reputation for everyone, not just users.
5 True
6 False. Product positioning aims to ensure that a product has unique and distinguishing features, appealing to particular consumers.
7 False. Industrial marketing is marketing of goods and services between companies. It contrasts with consumer marketing, which targets individual consumers.
8 True

Test 53

A

1 Price and promotional factors
2 external factors
3 buyer factors
4 needs
5 supplier factors

B

1 discounts
2 terms
3 trade fairs
4 trade journals
5 purchasing policy
6 stock levels
7 after-sales service
8 labour relations

Test 54

A

1 c	3 e	5 a
2 d	4 f	6 b

B

1 domestic
2 strength
3 weakness, supplier
4 overseas
5 buyers
6 supply, demand
7 free market economy
8 global, local

Test 52

Behaviouristic segmentation	**Benefits segmentation**	**Demographic segmentation**
use/non-use of product	product characteristics	age
knowledge/awareness of a product	product performance	sex
attitudes to a product		ethnic origin
		nationality

Geographic segmentation	**Industrial market segmentation**	**Psychographic segmentation**
state/country	turnover	opinions
urban/suburban/rural	type of company	political beliefs
region	size of company	leisure interests
climate		

Test 55
1 Same
2 Different. A client buys a service; a customer buys a product.
3 Same
4 Different. A survey investigates a market; a trend is the direction something is moving in, e.g. sales.
5 Different. The marketing mix is all aspects of marketing; the advertising mix is the combination of different advertising techniques.
6 Different. Product mix is the variety of products on offer from a certain company; the marketing mix is the combination of factors involved in how a company markets itself.
7 Same
8 Different. Opportunities are positive; threats are negative.
9 Different. A royalty is a commission paid on the number of sales; a franchise agreement is an agreement to use a famous product identity, logo, name, marketing approach, etc.
10 Same
11 Same
12 Different. Accounting is the job of looking after, preparing and presenting company accounts or finances. Accountability is the obligation to meet certain standards that society expects.

Test 56
1 economies of scale
2 marketing audit
3 marketing planning
4 external audit
5 economies of scope
6 marketing research
7 public sector, service
8 competition, accountability

Test 57
1 b	4 c	7 a
2 b	5 a	8 b
3 c	6 a	9 c

Test 58
Countries: **Mexico and Chile**
Preferred expansion method: overseas agents and distributors
Advantages: effective, cheap
Possible difficulties: conflict of interest if agent also sells competitor's products
Recommendation: set up sole distribution agreements

Countries: **Peru and Bolivia**
Preferred expansion method: franchising, joint ventures or other partnerships
Advantages: common in food and drinks industry, less capital intensive
Sources of income: license payments and other fees from franchisee

Country: **Argentina**
Preferred expansion method: international marketing strategy, setting up manufacturing and sales subsidiaries
Advantages: full integration in target market
Main disadvantages: very capital intensive, risky
Recommendations: carry out detailed market research, run subsidiaries as cost centres

Test 59
1 True
2 False. Usually the opposite: to drop them, spend no money.
3 True. Stars can make good short term profits and may become Cash Cows, therefore producing long term profits.
4 True
5 True
6 True
7 False – Strategic Business Unit
8 True
9 False – it looks at individual product areas, or even individual products.
10 False – the text does not say this. Anyway, the SBU approach can be used in manufacturing or in service industries, and in the private or public sector.

Test 60
1 domestic		5 external audit
2 marketing audit		6 threat
3 SWOT analysis		7 export
4 internal audit		8 trend

Word list

The numbers after the entries are the tests in which they appear.

A

above-the-line promotion 35
access code 27
accountability 55, 56
accountable 26
accounting 55
achiever 50
action plan 5
added value 6, 7, 15
advance orders 19
advertisement 3, 34
advertising 3, 16, 32, 36, 52, 53
advertising (planning) 34, 59
advertising budget 59
advertising campaign 34
advertising mix 34, 55
advertising research 40
after-sales assistance 14
after-sales service 12, 53
agency research 41
agent 20, 24, 30, 58
aggressive pricing 19
AIDA 35
air freight transportation 25
analyst 3
analysis (of research data) 43
appeal 13
application (of research results) 43
assets 49
attitude 44, 47
augmented package 12
augmented product 9, 11

B

banking 26, 28
banner towing 32
barge 25
behaviour 47
behaviouristic segmentation 52
belonger 50
below-the-line promotion 35
benefits segmentation 52
bias 39, 42, 46
billboard 32
BOGOF 37
Boston Consulting Group (BCG) 59
brand 10
brand identity 9, 10

brand image 10
brand loyalty 16, 48
brand name 9, 10, 29, 54
brand strength 10, 54
brand valuation 10
branding 10
break-even point 19, 22
browsing 27
budget priced goods 18, 20, 21
buyer 54
buyer behaviour 48, 49
buyer confidence 51
buyer factors 53
buyer's experience 53
buyers' market 5
buying decisions 53
buying direct 24
buying group 28
buying organisation 53

C

campaign 4, 34
cannibalism 9
capital investment 58
cargo plane 25
cartel 22
cash cow 59
cash investment 59
catalogue 29, 34
causal research 41
chain stores 28
chains 29
civil servants 42
client 49, 55
climate 52
clinical trial 41, 42
clone 11
closed question 42, 45
cluster sampling 44, 45
cold calling 28, 37
command economy 54
commercial 33, 34
commercial buying 54
commission 23, 28
commission agent 30
communication 33
communication skills 26
company valuation 10